WHAT READERS ARE SAYING...

"I work as a librarian in an elementary school where I see many shy children struggle to fit in. Teachers and parents are looking for a way to help shy children do their best to succeed. *Don't Call Me Shy* is a warm, easy-to-use book that helps shy children learn to become social.

"As a librarian I have yet to find a book that offers such good sound advice specifically on how to help shy children succeed. What an important difference it makes to read a book on shyness written by a parent who has gone through raising a shy child and who gives advice from a realistic point of view. Laurie Adelman is so in tune with the needs and feelings of shy children that I have a new respect and softness for how it is to be shy.

"The Skill Builder chapter is chock full of confidence-building techniques that have shy children feeling absolutely terrific about how special they are and what they can accomplish.

"*Don't Call Me Shy* should be mandatory reading for parents of shy children and all teachers in every school district in the country. Shy children need this book!"

—Judy Vanderweil
School librarian / media specialist

"This well written and easy-to-read book gives multiple techniques and step-by-step activities to help parents bring out the social best in their child. I heartily recommend it."

—Elliot M. Eisenstein, M.D., F.A.A.P.
Chairman, Department of Pediatrics
St. Joseph's Wayne Hospital

"*Don't Call Me Shy* reads like a how-to book for raising socially successful children. This book contains many practical tools for parents, but considering the amount of time that our children spend in a school setting, *Don't Call Me Shy* should be required reading for aspiring and existing teachers. Although we think of schools primarily as academic institutions, there can be no denying that the bulk of a child's socialization skills are being developed and rigorously tested there as well. *Don't Call Me Shy* clearly brings to light the ways in which a teacher's attitudes about, perceptions of, and responses to shy students can have a make-or-break effect on whether these students can reach their true potential and become both socially and academically successful individuals. I have introduced some of the techniques from *Don't Call Me Shy* into my classroom and, already, I have seen positive change!"

—Laura Hoogstrate, B.S.
Elementary Education

"*Don't Call Me Shy* offers parents and educators an understanding of those children who need extra support and encouragement to make their way in a social setting. The author gives us an in-depth look at the behaviors that lead to the 'shy' label and the negative impact that has on any child's self esteem.

"*Don't Call Me Shy* provides a variety of scenarios – familiar to many of us – and then provides practical tools to help any youngster who is painfully reluctant to participate in an activity.

"Ms. Adelman's advice is on target because it comes from personal experience. This book is an important guide to helping our children succeed in any social arena."

—Barbara Zitcer, Director, Early Childhood Dept.
YM-YWHA of North New Jersey

"Laurie Adelman writes a sensitive and practical guide that will assist parents, teachers, or anyone who cares for children. The author has a way of touching the reader in a very understanding manner, and I found myself laughing and crying as she described situations that I, too, had gone through. I came away from the book singing the 'Social Me' song, a technique that helps shy children remember the steps they must take each time they find themselves in a social situation.

Don't Call Me Shy is a very important book that makes it easy for caretakers to help shy children achieve social comfort in an upbeat and positive manner. As a first grade teacher and the mother of shy daughters, I wish I had had *Don't Call Me Shy* to rely on for valuable guidance and support."

—Florence Polay, M.S.
Elementary Education

DON'T CALL ME SHY

DON'T CALL ME SHY

PREPARING SHY CHILDREN FOR A LIFETIME OF SOCIAL SUCCESS

LAURIE ADELMAN

LANGMARC
PUBLISHING
AUSTIN, TEXAS

Don't Call Me Shy

Preparing Shy Children for a Lifetime of Social Success

Laurie Adelman

Cover Graphics: Michael Qualben

Published by

LangMarc Publishing

Trade book publisher
P.O. Box 90488
Austin, Texas 78709

Library in Congress PCN: 2007928707

ISBN: 9781-880292-327

DEDICATION

This book is dedicated to my daughter Becky
and other shy children
who CAN move from shy to social
when parents and grandparents,
teachers and friends
hear their plea:
"Don't Call Me Shy."

May you all find the strength
and wisdom in these pages to try…

CONTENTS

FOREWORD

Laurie Adelman offers a practical step-by-step program for nurturing social confidence in children. This well-written book is a powerful resource for helping liberate the social potential of a shy child.

Don't Call Me Shy focuses on the inner self-talk of a shy child. That voice says, "I'm shy and I can't be social with people." Adelman maintains that this inner voice becomes a stigmatizing block to a child's personal potential. That self-talk is a reflection of the labeling messages the child hears from her parent and other caregivers: "Why are you so shy? Say hello." Such labeling needs to be countered with responses that do not promote anxiety in a shy child but offer optimism for future social success. "You need a little time to get used to new situations, and it's okay."

The author talks about her own experience growing up as a shy child and raising her daughter, who also was shy. These personal disclosures add warmth and interest to a book that is filled with no-nonsense practical advice for parents to help their shy child. Parents will learn about methods for training their child in "good friend making" (GFM) behaviors. The GFM skill helps a child change her inner self-talk from "I can't" to "I can." Parents learn how to implement a program called "YOU CAN DO IT," which supports their child's efforts towards achieving social comfort. Parents also learn how to teach their child to make that effort using the "READY, SET, GO, Social Readiness Program."

As a psychotherapist specializing in parent and child relationships, I recommend this book to parents who complain about their child's social anxiety.

Don't Call Me Shy has much to offer in treating a condition that limits a child's ability to be her best now and tomorrow.

John DeMarco, M.Ed., LPC

PREFACE

One day many years ago, a little girl nicknamed Leah awoke with a start. Today was her birthday party, but instead of looking forward to a day filled with joyful anticipation and fun, she was preoccupied with thoughts that did not allow her mind to rest. Her parents had insisted on inviting her entire class to her party, even though Leah told them that she had only one friend named Kate. In fact, Kate really did not count as a true friend because the two girls had never spoken, but, oh how Leah longed to be Kate's friend!

The truth was that Leah was pretty sure that Kate wanted to be her friend, too. The week before, Kate had smiled at her when the two girls were taking their coats off in the cubby area. Leah did not have the courage to smile back, though. Instead, she looked away. Leah never felt as lonely and sad as she had at that moment.

"Why am I always so shy?" Leah asked the darkness. Abruptly her thoughts raced back to the present. "Nobody understands how I feel. I don't want a birthday party. I'm just going to act the same old shy way that I always do, and mommy and daddy will be disappointed in me...again."

Leah hugged the covers tightly in an effort to safely seal herself off from the world. Here was a child just turning eight who felt hopeless. Would life ever be any better?

I can relate this story with vivid detail because this child was me.

Shy children should never go through what I did. Parents and teachers can help these wonderful children grow to feel comfortable in social situations by using a specific method that transforms a shy child into a social child.

I know that social growth is possible because I accomplished it. You, too, can give a shy child in your life the priceless gift of social comfort. I will share with you what I have learned for myself—a formula for social success.

Teachers and shy adults, prior to reading Chapter One, can refer to the Appendix where you will find information pertaining to your specific needs.

Although I use the term "shy" throughout the book, I do so for clarity's sake only. In my interactions with children, the shy word is never used. I strongly suggest that you never use the term either.

The female gender is used when referring to both girls and boys. This allows the text to flow smoothly and remain consistent. Unless otherwise noted, all explanations apply equally to boys and girls.

To maintain privacy of the people described in this book, other than Becky and the author, any reference to a particular person is a composite of a number of individuals, and similarity to one particular person is purely coincidental.

ACKNOWLEDGMENTS

I am infinitely grateful to my daughter Becky for demonstrating, before my eyes, the benefits of the teachings of this book. She has grown to be a delightful young lady who is well on her way to achieving her social best.

My special thanks to Lois Qualben, president of LangMarc Publishing, for recognizing the importance of sharing the message in this book, and her warmth and enthusiasm that encouraged me to continue my work on this project until I had written a book that we could all be proud of.

Many words of thanks to the adults and children who shared their private, often painful, stories of how shyness affected their lives. Their experiences, good and bad, allowed me to fine-tune my techniques.

And a very special note of appreciation to my daughter, Melanie, who was my cheering section and showed such intense interest and excitement in my writing this book. Your love and inspiration kept me going.

Thanks to my husband, Jerry, who motivated me to continue in pursuit of my dream.

Laurie Adelman

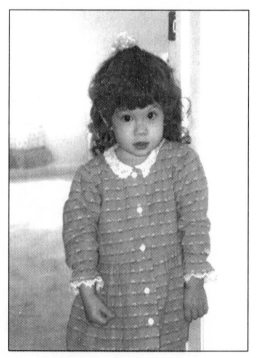

"But...please don't call me shy."

CHAPTER ONE

MUCH MORE THAN SHY

By changing the way you interact with your shy child, you can help her feel comfortable in social situations. If your goal is to change your shy child into an extrovert, please close this book. If, instead, you can envision your child becoming comfortable with who she is and how she behaves socially, then read on.

Consider this:

A baby just is.

A toddler is told by her parents what she is.

A child accepts what her parents tell her about herself without question.

An adult becomes what she believes she is capable of achieving.

The way parents define their child determines the way that the individual comes to define herself. Have you ever seriously thought about the effect that the word "shy" has on your child?

On a personal note

By sharing my personal journey toward social comfort, hopefully you will gain new insights into the mindset of your shy child. It is amazing that memories we hold onto from childhood remain vivid throughout our adult years. How we emerge as an adult is very much a function of how well we handled important life events. One memory lies very close to my heart.

At age six and in the first grade, I was asked to draw a picture of myself and write a sentence that best described me. I carefully drew a detailed dress on a very sad-looking little girl. In rudimentary lettering, I printed the most meaningful expression of my life:

i AM SHY

What is so significant about this experience is that I could have described myself with any of the following terms:

KIND
FUNNY
SMART

Instead, I wrote the words
with which I defined myself.

At age six, I had labeled myself long before I even knew what a label was. Early into adolescence I thought of myself as shy first, followed by all of my other more meaningful characteristics. Throughout my childhood and young adulthood, I longed to express my desire to be recognized for who I really was.

It was not until high school that I began to slowly evolve into a multifaceted individual. I became my own cheering section, and in my determination to become all that I was capable, the layers of shyness were shed until the never-before-seen genuine me emerged. When I allowed my true self to flow forth, something wonderful happened. I realized I was not merely shy, but that I also possessed charm, wit, and enthusiasm. For the first time in my life, I experienced a feeling of limitless potential. The happiness and pride in myself was overwhelming.

CHARM
WIT
ENTHUSIASM

These attributes had been hidden beneath my shyness label, and the flow of my true potential had been blocked. I came to see that I was much more than shy, and the possibilities for self-expression were endless. My journey toward social comfort had begun.

On being shy

Being shy was an awful secret that I tried to hide. People and social situations were to be avoided. After all, I was not good enough, but the tools to do better were not available to me. My mother did her best, but she did not know how to cope with my shyness. My perception was that she was ashamed of the way I behaved. Even when she wasn't with me, her stinging words that labeled me "Oh you're so shy" hung over my head like a heavy black cloud.

I imagined that people could see clear through me and knew of my discomfort while I thought everyone else was totally at ease. With one look, one gesture, which may not have even been directed at me, I perceived that others were disappointed in me just as my mother had been. I felt disappointed in myself. My mind repeated over and over, "You're so shy. You can't talk to people." And the more that I focused on these thoughts, the less able I was to do something about my behavior.

Oh to have a mentor, someone to praise me for all of the untapped potential that lay dormant within me. I needed a parent to offer me some well-founded guidelines to help me approach my social challenges. My need was for the very parent that I am going to help you become for your child.

A note to parents (along with a hug)

Writing this book proved to be an emotional roller coaster because I was forced to remember how difficult it was for me growing up. As a shy adolescent, I recognized what I needed to do to bring about my full potential. I did it on my own and without the advice or support of anyone.

The answer came from within, and fortunately I had the strength and fortitude to carry it out. From the shadow of shyness, insecurity, and low self-esteem, a socially comfortable individual was born—a challenging process, to be sure.

The ideal time to intervene is during childhood. Life truly works in mysterious and wonderful ways. When my daughter Becky was born, it was not long before I realized she was a shy child. She had many of the same characteristics that I possessed as a child. My mission in life was to do everything possible to help this wonderful child see she was much more than shy.

Certain things in life occur for a reason. I was placed in a situation where I had full responsibility for raising a shy child and viewed this gift as my second chance. An environment for my child could be created that was conducive to the development of her full social potential. Repairs upon the life I had led could be made and the results could be assessed as I went along. What resulted is the method I propose for your child.

When asked to draw a picture and describe herself at age six, Becky scrolled the following words underneath a detailed picture of a happy-looking child:

i am great at sharing
and being a good friend

Even though Becky has some of the characteristics one may regard as shy, it would not occur to her to describe herself in this manner. Becky has come to know and appreciate herself and is realistically aware of how she feels in various situations. She has an accepting attitude toward herself and is very much her own person. Today, Becky at age 11 likes herself and is genuinely proud of who she is. This is a great accomplishment at any age and probably the greatest gift we can give to our children.

If all of this sounds too good to be true for your shy child, note that Becky was what most would consider extremely shy up until she was five. A major difference in upbringing from most other shy children was that we never called her "shy." As a result, Becky did not learn to see herself as shy and, therefore, did not become so.

By applying my parenting techniques, our daughter has grown to be a self-assured rather feisty young lady.

From the mouth of babes

When Becky was four years old, we took her to the circus. Before the show started, a clown kneeled down beside her, and Becky jumped into my arms. "Shy, are you?" asked the clown. Without missing a beat, and in a tone that was far louder than her usual voice, Becky shouted "Don't call me shy!" The entire audience began to clap, but nobody felt prouder than I did because Becky had uttered the words that every shy child wishes they had the courage to say. Don't call me shy. Words that are far too important to ignore.

Helping you parent your child

As a nurse and an educator, I have agonized over my own shy child enough to realize there is need for assistance and sound advice on how best to handle such a child. My goal is to help you make parenting of a shy child a more joyful, less anxiety-ridden activity. I have attempted to do what was best for my child in a world that generally frowns upon who she is. Here is a combination of valid and practical advice, psychological and philosophical understanding, and empathy to you, the parent who struggles daily with the challenges of how best to raise your child.

A non-judgmental positive approach to shyness

Just as it is devastating to define your child as shy, it is equally damaging to set up a goal that is unrealistic. We will do neither. Our focus will be on behavior, not on labels and put-downs. You will learn techniques that offer praise and encouragement to bring out the potential that lies dormant within your child.

You will help your child see herself clearly in very specific ways. Through various steps and exercises, you will equip your child with the tools necessary to effectively deal with any social situation.

Having mastered my methods, your child will have a better chance of going through life with a consistent feeling of self pride and self worth no matter what social environment she finds herself.

Parents of shy children cope with many emotional ups and downs. I have cried myself to sleep more than once after seeing my three year old sit off to the side at preschool or watching her want desperately to tell a funny story to a friend but not being ready to do so. And my heart swelled with pride the first time my daughter felt able to walk into the birthday party room all by herself, the time she asked another child to play, and the day she read aloud in front of her entire class. Parents of shy children know how powerful these steps can be.

The successes grew as my Becky grew. I watched my dear girl go on her first sleep over. Attending summer day camp led to the day when Becky asked if she could go to sleep-away camp. Weekly dance class led to her performing on stage in front of four hundred people. Teachers who did not know Becky before age eight are astounded to hear that this self-assured, full of fun, rather outgoing child was ever shy.

This book is written for every child who struggles with the desire to speak out. My approach reaches out to the youngster who wants to play at recess but just doesn't know how to get involved. You will learn how to help the little girl who plans on talking to another child in class but can't muster up the courage to start the conversation. Parents and teachers need to understand what it is like to be the young girl or boy who plays ball really well at home but doesn't yet know how to approach the other children at school. Parents like me who want to do all that you can to help your own shy child succeed can become an expert at bringing out your child's social best.

MY THEORY

We become who we think we are.

What a child believes about herself causes her to behave that very way.

We can change the way that we think about ourselves.

A child's thoughts about herself in a given situation directly determine how she will behave. Therefore, when she changes her thoughts, she will create new behaviors.

The way in which a parent labels a child is the same way that the child will label herself. Label her shy and that is how she will view herself.

Once a child develops a concept of herself as being shy, she will not question whether or not this is true. She will behave in a manner that is consistent with her label.

Although the potential toward shyness may be inborn, this does not dictate that any child must remain shy.

If a child initially displays shy characteristics she can learn to behave in other, more socially comfortable ways.

How a parent labels a child will either create a feeling of positive or negative self-worth.

The choice as to how a child is labeled is the parent's responsibility.

When we create opportunities for success, this gives the child the confidence to continue to try.

A person grows to feel capable when she experiences positive outcomes. When we want our child to feel that she is capable of social success, we must put her in situations that enable her to experience social success.

The word "should" is a dangerous term when it is used with regard to the actions of a child.

"Should" implies that the child has failed according to a certain set of standards that have been decided upon without her consultation.

By creating a positive atmosphere in which to grow, a child will blossom into an individual that both parent and child will be immensely proud.

When a parent creates an accepting, positive atmosphere within the home, everyone within the family thrives.

CHAPTER TWO

A NEW APPROACH TO SHYNESS

My path has been a tough battle, and I was left to find my own way. The shy label presented an ongoing challenge to me for as long as I can remember. In fact, shyness has overshadowed everything I have encountered and accomplished in my life. The subject of shyness has always fascinated me on a personal level as well as a scientific one.

To further understand my life experiences, I earned a Bachelor of Science degree in Community Health Nursing and a Masters degree in Family Health and Health Education. I have worked on bits and pieces of this book all of my life. As a nursing student, I would sit at a playground for hours and observe the interaction between children and adults.

Over a period of 25 years, I spoke with thousands of parents and children and wrote pages of notes. Preschool and elementary school principals and hundreds of teachers were interviewed, and they discussed with me how they approached a shy child. I devoured everything I could get my hands on concerning self-esteem, child development, and shyness.

Answers to two important questions were sought: What actions on the part of caretakers appeared to bring about social ease with more reserved children? and What interactive style appeared to do damage to a child's comfort level? My lifelong research and the raising of my own shy daughter taught me that there was, indeed, a parenting technique that brought out the social best in shy children.

When I shared my observations and stories of success in dealing with shyness, the typical response was "You should write a book." or "Other parents out there would love to hear what you have to say." "You have done it yourself; why not share with others what you have accomplished."

Some of my most meaningful encounters were with teachers who had shy children of their own. "Here I am a teacher, and even I don't know what to do to help my students or my own shy child." "Your approach is not only one of a kind, but it offers compassion and understanding for the child as well as the parent." A school librarian exclaimed, "Write your ideas in a book and send it to every school district in the country. Shy children need you!"

What I had lived and learned enabled me to offer a brand new approach taken from the vantage point of the shy child as well as the parent of such a child.

Being a parent is challenging

As parents, we want what is best for our children

and most of us do all we can. Parenting requires very specific knowledge and guidelines. There isn't a parent who would argue that child rearing is probably the most difficult job there is. We look for well-founded facts that we can abide by with confidence. Parents of shy children need a guidebook focused on their needs.

A so-called shy child presents a specific set of circumstances that creates a unique and sometimes overwhelming challenge. My approach to parenting a shy child goes against much of what we think about when we hear the word shy. Even though no two people are shy in the exact same way, the shy word groups a list of mostly undesirable characteristics into one word—"shy," which sets up your child for failure before she even starts. Avoid using the word shy because this word does far more harm than good.

As a little girl, my mother gave me the impression that, because of my shyness, I did not live up to what she expected of me. For much of my life, I compared myself to my mother's notion of what I was supposed to be. I always fell short as far as my social abilities were concerned. It took me many years to realize that, in fact, having unrealistic expectations for our child is unfair and damaging. When parents come to expect too much of their child or fail to pay attention to the child's specific needs, the child feels like a failure because she compares herself to an ideal that is unrealistic for her.

My approach to parenting a shy child is aimed at redefining the word shy for your child and for yourself. You will learn how to work with your child's specific set of needs to help her function more comfortably and confidently in social situations and to ultimately recognize and appreciate who she really is. By changing your approach and fine-tuning your expectations for your child, she will come to create realistic possibilities for herself.

A key feature of this book is my direct focus on you, the parent. Specific techniques are discussed that you can directly apply to your child. You will learn to create a home environment that will be conducive to learning. An atmosphere of warmth will result when you institute my program and will bubble over into all parent-child interactions. While you experience pride in your child's new-found social abilities, she will enjoy the encouraging feedback you focus upon her. A true metamorphosis will occur in both of you.

Take the time you need

To become an expert in the growth of your child's social potential, you will need to make a serious investment in terms of time and effort. This book will outline specific parenting techniques. Theory is presented before approach so that you have the opportunity to understand fundamental background information before applying it. You will come to understand how it is that children learn in the first place and what mechanisms can be implemented to bring about desirable behavior. Take the time you need to master the skills that are presented. Some chapters may seem uncomplicated, while others may require a few days to a week to fully comprehend.

Just as you will need to invest quite a bit of time in this venture, the same is true for your child. Sometimes we parents are so excited to witness positive results from a new approach that if the desired behavior does not occur immediately we conclude the program is not working. In reality, any new idea must be given a fair chance to take hold.

Change in your child will not occur overnight, particularly in the older child who already has developed a self concept that tells her she is shy. Since it has taken her whole life to form her idea of a shy self, it will take some time to change these ideas. It is never too late, though, to begin to increase the ease by which your child conducts herself in a social manner.

If your child is three or four years old, you are in an ideal situation to apply these principles because you can help your child form a positive social self image right from the start. Rest assured that important changes are taking place in your child's mind even if you are not yet able to see them. The first and most important step in changing social behavior is to help your child form a belief system that tells her she has the ability to comfortably function in the social arena. Once this is accomplished, you will introduce techniques to bring about lasting changes in your child's behavior. Be patient and you will be amazed how far your child can progress.

We all learn by repetition. We need to experience ideas repeatedly in order for them to become part of our behavioral repertoire. Both you and your child need to proceed at your own pace. Remember that everything worthwhile in this world requires time to develop, for all good things come to those who wait.

Best of luck. Before getting down to the specifics of how to develop optimal social abilities in your shy child, it is important that you consider the following question: *What are we doing to our children?*

Chapter Three

What Are We Doing to Our Children?

"Shy, shy, shy," her mind repeated.
"I'm such a failure. I feel so stupid."
No child should ever feel this way.

It was visiting day at school. All of the parents were crowded into fifth grade classroom number seven. The children were taking turns speaking about books they had read.

It was Alyssa's turn.

"Alyssa," the teacher said with a smile.

Alyssa stood and inched her way to the front of the room. Her face was beet red, and she swallowed repeatedly. Her mind felt cloudy, and her thoughts were garbled.

"I CAN'T do this," she thought.

Her head pounded as those all too familiar words echoed in her brain. "Shy, shy, shy."

"Let's get started," the teacher prompted.

In a voice that was barely audible, Alyssa mouthed some words.

She tried again to speak while her hands shook uncontrollably.

Her classmates were getting fidgety.

All eyes were glued in her direction, willing her to go on.

Alyssa felt out of control.

She could feel the tension in the room. Everyone could.

Alyssa looked down once more and whispered the final words of her report. She was finished!

Feelings of relief intermingled with feelings of embarrassment and an overwhelming intense notion of failure consumed her. This certainly was not the first time that she felt this way.

"Shy, shy, shy," her mind repeated.

"I'm such a failure. I feel so stupid."

The teacher's words jarred Alyssa from her private thoughts.

"Okay," the teacher said. "Are there any questions from the class?"

Immediately a hand shot up from the front of the room.

"Yes, Joey," the teacher said.

"I couldn't hear one stinkin' word of her report," he said with disgust.

Alyssa's pain was palpable.

Alyssa's mother sat with tears streaming down her face, wringing her hands.

The school day was over.

Alyssa rushed out through the doors of the classroom.

"Mom," she cried, looking down.

"I couldn't do it...again!" she proclaimed.

"I know," replied her mother, hugging her tightly.

"Speaking in front of the class is just not for you. You're too shy."

The shy word bellowed in Alyssa's head, making it less and less likely that she would ever be able to comfortably speak in front of her class.

"Shy, shy, shy, shy, shy, shy, shy, shy!"

This is the inner voice of the shy child. It reminds her daily that she is shy, but much more damaging, it reminds her over and over again of what she *cannot* do. The shy word becomes a code or a type of shorthand for other more destructive labels.

Shy quickly gets translated into terms such as failure, no good, stupid, and embarrassment. Here forms the destructive mental foundation for the shy child's life.

Being labeled as shy, a child is, in effect, given a list of behaviors that she is supposedly unable to do.

Shy means
CAN'T

"I can't be friendly, I can't speak to others, I can't make friends, I can't answer in class…"

The most meaningful moment of my life

There is probably a single moment in every person's life where his or her mind becomes clearly focused and certain ideas make perfect sense. We are never the same person again, and thoughts that we gathered all of our life come together and clearly reveal their meaning. The events that took place in classroom number seven represents that moment for me. As an ex-shy person myself and the parent of a shy child, I was so moved by what I witnessed that day that I was driven to further understand what had taken place.

You see, I was one of those parents sitting in the back of the classroom. I was there to observe my own child, yet my thoughts and my heart were engulfed by Alyssa's pain. Throughout my childhood I, too, had listened to the monotony of my own internal voice screaming to me that I was shy. I listened for years to an ongoing list in my head of what I could not do because I was shy. The feeling of helplessness was overwhelming as I shared the hurt of this damaged child named Alyssa, and I vividly recalled what the shy label had done to me.

My first eye-opening glimpse into my own life story was when I viewed some amateur movies that my father had taken when I was a child. As a baby I was often smiling, warm, and open. I seemed to prefer close family members and balked in the arms of my aunt, yet I was happy. As a toddler I appeared quite content, often singing and dancing before the camera. When age five rolled around, my demeanor had undergone a drastic change; I had developed into a quiet, withdrawn, and serious child. Gone were the spontaneous antics before the lens. Lost was my enthusiasm. Home movies of me at this age pictured a reserved, seemingly sad subject. What had happened to the spark that I previously had within? Why, at age five, had my gusto dissipated? And most urgent of questions, why had my personality changed at all? For weeks I tortured myself with these questions. A bolt of reality struck as it occurred to me that at age five I began to identify myself as shy.

History had repeated itself with Alyssa, a beautiful child who was totally unaware of how wonderful she really was. As was my case, all she had been taught to see was her shyness. She did what was expected by her parents, her teachers, her relatives, and herself. She fulfilled her role as shy. As I observed ten-year-old Alyssa, I was looking at ten-year-old me. Alyssa, too, was experiencing the profound negative effects of shyness. No child should ever be allowed to feel that way. Happily, there is another side to each shy soul that eagerly awaits our recognition. All we need do is look.

The other side of shyness...

Here lies all of the hidden possibilities that remain dormant under the self-limiting disguise of the shy word. Without proper guidance and support, the true internal beauty of the individual fails to shine through. The only aspect that blooms forth is the shyness. Inside and out, the child defines herself with this potential-stopping term. Shy, shy, shy. The word takes over like a cancer to invade every aspect of life. When we allow this to happen, full potential fails to blossom, and the world never gets an opportunity to see all that this individual is capable of becoming.

It has become excruciatingly clear to me that we parents are carrying out an incredible injustice by mislabeling our children as shy. Yes **mis**labeling, for the term represents a microscopically small portion of what a person can be. Throughout the years, I have come to hold a strong conviction that the creation of the shy child comes from accepting these negative thoughts. When we treat our child as though we expect that she will behave in a shy manner, indeed she does. Most parents believe that a child is either shy or not shy and that is that. We don't bother to look any deeper, but we must.

Babies are born free

The most distressing fact to me about labeling is that nobody is born with this negative tool. Babies just love themselves. Not one of them ever considers that they are anything but wonderful. Even toddlers adore everything about themselves. They don't entertain the thought that there is anything that they cannot do! That is, until we tell them otherwise.

When the child hits four or five years old, the party's over. Here comes the sad transition, for now the child begins to understand the judgment of adults. Where the child has painted herself rosy, we tell her to color gray for it is here that we teach our child how to see herself from *our* point of view. We put forth our expectations for her, and we let her know where she is not measuring up. It is at this time that our child learns to question the wonder of her very being. If we see that our child is not as outgoing as we would like, we teach her the shy word and then define it for her in a most damaging way. The most remarkable thing is that most of us don't even realize the mess that we are creating. It is time, long overdue, to reexamine what we are doing to our children.

What have we done to Alyssa?

Many of us know or have an Alyssa of our own. Few of us have been given the tools to educate our shy child or ourselves! If you have wrestled with the idea of shyness in yourself or you are concerned about your own child, now is the time to open your eyes and your heart. Shyness is a very destructive label that we have been pinning on our children for much too long. It is time to change our approach.

When we label, we tend to think of our child in absolute terms. This is our shy child. How else could we expect her to behave because, after all, she is shy. Then we define for our child the limited amount of possibilities that we expect of her. These labels become the very goals that she comes to expect for herself. How limiting! How inaccurate! How unfair!

It is time to stop labeling and explore the idea of potential so that you can learn to help your child create endless possibilities for herself.

CHAPTER FOUR

THE WONDERFUL CONCEPT
OF POTENTIAL

*Most of us develop only a small portion of our
potential because we are never given the belief that
there is much more there to develop.*

*Help your child define herself as having many
abilities, and new traits appear to develop before your
eyes.*

It is fascinating to look at individuals who grow to
develop a personality that is entirely different from
what anyone would have originally thought. Nowhere
is it written that any of us are destined to behave in one
particular way. The potential for our personal development is infinite and is directly related to how we come to
see ourselves.

The life of Eleanor Roosevelt is a study in the wonder
of potential. As a child, Eleanor showed shy char-

acteristics and came to feel socially uncomfortable because she believed that she could not measure up to the outgoing behavior of the family members who surrounded her. Instead of being encouraged by her mother, Eleanor was frequently told that her shyness was an embarrassment. The shy word followed her everywhere and Eleanor came to define herself in this manner. Eleanor's life was a whirlwind of parties and social functions, all of which served to reinforce in her mind that she was shy. She tried to avoid as many social interactions as she could and became quite withdrawn at an early age. Eleanor probably would have continued a shy existence if it were not for two role models who greatly influenced her social outcome.

A teacher helped build confidence

Eleanor was blessed to have a teacher who took a very special interest in her. This fine soul must have recognized the potential that lay dormant within this child, for she began to praise and encourage her every chance that she could. To help her develop confidence, the teacher made it Eleanor's job to dismiss the class. Her fellow students were instructed to wait for Eleanor's signal before they were permitted to leave the lunch-room. With time, Eleanor began to view herself as a leader and the other students looked up to her. To further build confidence as she grew older, the teacher designated Eleanor to be in charge of more and more responsibilities, including making travel arrangements and purchasing tickets.

With each task accomplished you can envision the shedding of the shyness label and its replacement with another more appropriate term. As time progressed, Eleanor no longer felt socially inadequate. She was on her way to expressing her full social potential. What a major impact this innovative teacher had upon this impressionable child!

An uncle recognized potential

Lucky for Eleanor, she had another individual who played an extremely important role in unleashing her full potential. Early on, Eleanor's Uncle Ted became a strong figure in her life. Ted was well aware of Eleanor's shy behavior, but he, like her teacher, was able to look beyond the shyness. This loving uncle saw similar characteristics in Eleanor to ones that he possessed. Both embodied a fighting spirit, a term Ted used to refer to the fact that each had the ability to accomplish what they set their mind to doing. Uncle Ted proudly referred to Eleanor's fighting spirit often, and he let her know that he saw something very positive within her that she could further develop and be proud of.

Through his loving guidance, Ted encouraged Eleanor to try her best and to take chances when confronted by something new, even though initially she felt afraid to do so. Given all of this encouragement, Eleanor stopped focusing on her shy behavior and began to see herself in a brand new light. Following each success, Eleanor became stronger and more sure of herself.

It would be difficult for someone who did not know her past to guess that Mrs. Eleanor Roosevelt, First Lady to President Franklin Delano Roosevelt, was ever shy at all. During the Great Depression, Eleanor visited factories and coal mines. Through her kind and friendly ways, she touched the lives of many, often lecturing before large groups (yes, very large groups), and entertaining world leaders.

As you may have guessed, Uncle Ted was known to most of us as President Theodore Roosevelt. This learned man had a sense of what it was that a shy child needed, and he was there to provide words of wisdom and love. Eleanor came to cherish the loving stories that Ted would relate of his own childhood, which contained monumentally important lessons for his beloved niece. (You, too, will learn how to become a motivational story teller, and how this technique can help you mentor your own shy child.)

If it were not for the understanding of her wonderful teacher and uncle, the world may never have had the opportunity to benefit from all that Eleanor had to offer. As a young child only a small portion of her personality was expressed. But as others recognized Eleanor's potential and offered loving support, she became aware of characteristics that she never knew she had. For deep within this wonderful child, underneath the veil of shyness, the gift of friendliness and leadership began to flow forth. When you lift the veil of shyness from your own shy child and look carefully, you, too, will begin to see all that she is capable.

We look but fail to see

The analogy of looking through a peephole comes to mind. If we gaze through a peephole in a door, we are able to see only a small portion of what is on the other side.

Does this mean that what we see is all that exists? Of course not, for we miss what is outside our line of vision.

If we make judgments about what we see, we base our response only on a limited view. Now if we open the door, any conclusions that we make are based on the entire picture and are likely to be precisely accurate.

So is the case when we look at our shy child and focus only on the possibility of her acting shy. When we label her as such, we are gazing though the narrow peephole of shyness and only see the potential for shy behavior. We make judgments about our child based on incomplete information, and we transfer these limited expectations to our child.

Children believe what we tell them and accept these beliefs as true. It is a fact that children who do poorly in school and are classified in some way tend to think of themselves in this limited manner. Their teachers, their parents, and finally they themselves have very definite expectations of what they are capable and often fail to encourage and/or achieve behavior outside these beliefs.

Once upon potential

The beloved children's story *The Wizard of Oz* speaks directly to us about potential. Think about the lion. Throughout the story the lion is searching for courage, something he is sure that he does not possess. This supposedly cowardly creature is in search of a magical solution to his problem. He is off to see the wizard, an ordinary man who turns out to be brilliant. The wizard informs the beast that he has had courage all along but merely needed to believe it himself. With encouragement, the lion comes to see that he was courageous after all.

As with the lion, each shy child has the potential for positive social behavior. Through guidance and praise, we bring out the best in our children. Just as the cowardly lion was cowardly when he was labeled so, your shy child will remain shy if this is what she comes to expect of herself. If we act with the wisdom of the wizard, using specific guidelines to give our child the belief that she is capable, the yellow brick road to social comfort opens wide.

There is much that we can do to help or hinder our children from living up to their potential. Through our words and actions we transform our child. If an extremely talkative child is repeatedly told "be quiet, you never stop talking," this child is likely to feel that she doesn't have a lot of worthwhile things to say. She will probably never develop her full potential to be social. Along the same lines, if a child has the potential to be shy, yet she is helped to understand her nature and is given the tools to become more comfortable in social situations, she is likely to develop a positive feeling about herself and will shine with social ability.

The potential toward shyness

Potential means maybe, maybe not! The argument between whether or not shyness is inherited or is caused by an individual's upbringing is really a moot point.

Our child may be born with a tendency toward shyness, but this is merely a potential. The way in which we deal with our child throughout her formative years determines how much of her shy characteristics are realized. When we guide our children away from the self-limiting term of shyness and encourage her social potential, confidence soars.

A well-known psychologist named Jerome Kagan and his assistants studied temperament in an attempt to define the term shy. They felt that shy children were timid and fearful of anything new or strange. These researchers made the claim that shy individuals possessed nervous systems that reacted in a hypersensitive way. This type of thinking leads one to conclude that shy individuals are destined to remain shy.

Before you throw up your hands in resignation, consider a study that Kagan carried out in which a group of shy children and a group of their uninhibited peers were followed for the first eight years of their life. The results were truly telling. Most of the shy children continued to be shy just as most of the uninhibited children remained outgoing. Here is where it becomes really interesting, however. About 25 percent of the shy children became considerably more outgoing and a similar percentage of the uninhibited children became more hesitant and quiet. What was going on? After all, doesn't shy remain shy? The researchers attributed the changes to environmental factors. They reported that mothers of the shy children tried hard to get their children to be more outgoing while the uninhibited children were encouraged to behave in a quieter fashion.

This study hits like a train head-on, for we see that having the potential for shyness does not guarantee that it will remain so. So much power falls into the hands of parents to create an environment that fosters social ability. If 25 percent of the children in this study changed from shy children to what is seen as more outgoing individuals by parents who did not follow any specific set of guidelines, just imagine the potential for your child.

If you have always thought that being shy was purely inborn and that shy will remain shy, I urge you to let go of this misleading idea. This thought process is not only damaging to the way that you perceive your child, but it is death to the way that your child comes to see herself.

We all start off with endless potential

Babies are a squirming wonder of potential. All babies appear to be born with the potential for endless self-esteem. As a nurse, I have witnessed many babies coming into the world. Every newborn seems to be prepackaged with inborn feelings of self love. Each infant is different and approaches life with a unique sense of wonder, but all babies act as though they already know they are wonderful. A baby never wonders "Am I good enough?" Babies just "do," and in so doing, epitomize the outlook that we would all like to continue for our children.

If we all start out with this seemingly endless supply of self love, then what happens to all of this potential? The answer lies in how we socialize our children.

Babies grow into children who begin to listen to adults who tell them that they are not good enough the way that they are. They begin to lose these feelings of self love, which robs them of their ability to reach their full potential. Our goal must be to foster positive feelings in our children, thereby bringing out their best.

Give your child a choice of endless possibilities

Potential is a wonderful concept for it gives the individual the freedom to develop without being locked into any self-defeating label. Happily rewrite the word shy as potentially social. Allowing this small shift in terminology, we create a major change in attitude and give our child an infinite choice of wonderful possibilities. Unpin the label of shyness from your child and venture out onto a brand new road to social well being. Make it your goal for the word shy to become obsolete. Your child will begin to see herself in a whole new light as you view your child as potentially social. When you replace the word shy with potentially social, your child's expectations become focused on what she *can* do.

Your child is ready to work toward an attainable goal

Potentially social will boldly take the place of shy, along with an infinite amount of wonderful social possibilities. Potentially social implies that your child can behave other than in a shy manner. All of a sudden you are giving your child the opportunity to be social.

Shy means "I believe I CAN'T"
Potentially social means "I believe I CAN."

As a parent YOU determine whether your child will develop into a socially comfortable individual.

Help your child believe that SHE CAN...

CHAPTER FIVE

WHAT DO YOU BELIEVE
ABOUT YOURSELF?

Do you see yourself as capable or lazy?
Do you tend to be a leader or a follower?
Are you comfortable in social situations
or are you shy?
What impact did your parents have
upon who you are today?

The movie of your life

This exercise will help you understand the process
by which you form an opinion of yourself. Imagine that
you are viewing a film that features every detail of your
life up until today. Travel back in time and experience
the sights and sounds of your childhood. As you take in
these running images of yourself at various stages of
your life, pay particular attention to the messages that
you heard as a child. Were they words of understanding
and encouragement or were they critical?

Now fast forward to your adulthood. How many of the expectations that your parents had for you are true of yourself today? Have you changed very much throughout the years? If you are like most of us, the messages that were communicated to you as a child have probably remained with you into your adult years. It is likely that you turned out to be a very close approximation of what your parents told you you would become.

Remarkable, isn't it? You did what we all do: you listened to what your parents told you about what you were capable and accepted it.

The movie of your child's life

Once you have come to terms with this idea, abruptly change gears. This time imagine a movie of your child that begins with birth and continues right up until the present. Allow your heart to bond with your brand new baby, radiant and bursting with potential. Watch your child's story unfold until today. Carefully study the individual that lights up the screen....your child here and now.

How would you describe her behavior? Does the youngster before you appear to feel good about herself or does she project something else? Would you evaluate the behavior as socially comfortable or shy? And most important, what are the messages that your child receives about herself? Encouragement? Criticism? Pride? Disrespect?

Realize that each and every day, you create an ongoing movie of your child's life. While she is the actress, you represent the director, co-star, and choreographer. You exert a profound effect upon how your child feels about her own acting ability and how she interacts with the audience of her life. Yet up until today, only a small portion of your child's life has actually been played out. There is much more to be created.

You have tremendous power over the future of your child. You have the ability to create an environment that will enable your child to become the star in her own movie; the story of a shy child who grew to become socially comfortable. From this day forward, you will gently guide your child with methods to positively direct your child's lifetime course. And, as your producer, I will be with you every step of the way.

CHAPTER SIX

HOW OUR THOUGHTS AFFECT US

> "Whatever the mind can conceive and believe, it can achieve."
>
> Napoleon

I think, therefore I am

What we think about ourselves is what we actually become. If your child develops a thought pattern that says, "I am shy – I don't make friends easily," these thoughts produce feelings about herself. Your child accepts these feelings, internalizes them, and carries them around with her everywhere she goes and into each new situation that she faces. She comes to have shy expectations for herself. But suppose your child never internalizes thoughts of being shy and unfriendly. There is no preconceived notion of the way that she is expected to behave and endless possibilities remain.

Every time your child enters a social situation she has two ways of thinking:

"I CAN'T do it because I'm shy."
or
"I CAN do it when I try."

The power of language

We talk to ourselves all day long. This self-talk may be heard only in our mind, but the things that we say have much to do with how we feel about our abilities. When we feel capable, we speak to ourselves with encouraging words. If we see ourselves as incompetent, we talk in a negative way. When your child says to herself, "I can't because I am shy," her subconscious mind accepts these words along with a defeated feeling. She will be unable to picture any other options for herself. Your child's beliefs about herself keep her shy.

The language of negative thoughts

It is time to face an important truth. We parents take our spectacular toddler, and we rob her of some of the naturally good feelings that she was born with. We tell our child that she is not good enough, and we teach her a new dialogue that forever becomes a part of her internal thought pattern. We introduce our child to the language of negative thoughts.

Here your child learns that it was not okay for her to feel a little clingy at grandma's house, and it was not acceptable for her to refuse to say hello to your neighbor. We send her our feelings of disappointment, which leads, sooner or later, to her own feelings of disappointment in herself. Our child takes on the role of shy with dialogue that reads "there you go again, you shy unfriendly child. Why can't you play like other kids?"

Her negative vocabulary grows, and your child concludes, "I am not good enough. I am shy and I am not okay."

In a curious way, we pass on to our children not only our genes but also our expectations. We let our children know what we expect of them and our beliefs are translated into what they come to believe for themselves. Our thoughts make their way into our child's mind, and she forms ideas about what she can and cannot do. How you speak to your child has a direct effect on the way she will come to speak to herself.

Think about how damaging the shy word is to a child who is beginning to form her own self image. When a child is repeatedly told that she is shy, she will speak to herself as though she were shy, and that is the way she is sure to behave. Once a child is pinned with the label of shyness, all of her actions and emotions will be consistent with that label.

> The eight year old who doesn't even try to reach out to others believes he can't make friends because he is shy.

> The five year old who is told in kindergarten to "speak up and not be so shy" doesn't speak up because she knows that she can't because she is shy.

What our child believes she can accomplish is what she will actually accomplish.

The idea of believing in oneself is certainly not new. For years, athletes have used the notion of creative imaging to give themselves the competitive edge. When a swimmer pictures himself swimming particularly fast, these ideas become ingrained in his mind, and he is better able to achieve his goal. Gymnasts are known to mentally review every move just prior to their performance in order to perfect their routine. Researchers in the field of neurology actually believe that new pathways are created in the brain when an individual imagines herself behaving in a particular way.

Thoughts are powerful

I spoke with Sandy, a 35-year-old woman who, as a child, was told by her father that she was "too tall." Despite the fact that this woman ended up growing to a mere 5'3", she slouches terribly and never wears heels. As a child Sandy accepted false information about herself, and her mind continued to believe these ideas well into her adult years The way that Sandy's father spoke to her in childhood became the way that Sandy spoke to herself .

I am what I think I am

Henry Ford said, "If you think you can, you can and if you think you can't, you can't. Either way you are right." Along the same lines, if you think you're shy, you're shy, and if you think you're not, you're not. Either way you are right. Consider these statements very carefully because here lies the measure of your power as it relates to how profoundly you can affect your child. When we label our child as shy, we put an end to any potential social growth. We are telling our shy child that shy is all that she can expect to be, and that she has no control over her own behavior.

In a fascinating study done by researchers Jemmott and Gonzalez, fourth grade students were placed into groups of four. Each child was assigned to either a high-status or a low-status position. Here is how it was done:

The high-status children were given big attractive buttons to wear imprinted with the word BOSS.

The low-status children wore unimpressive buttons with the word helper written in tiny letters.

All groups of children had to unscramble a list of words. The words were on grade level and all of the children were similarly capable. What do you suppose occurred? Children who were labeled BOSS outperformed those who were labeled helper.

The children wearing the BOSS pin reasoned, "If I'm labeled BOSS, it means that I am expected to do well," and they did. The BOSS group lived up to their higher expectations. Help your child believe that she has the ability to become a social BOSS and you encourage her to reach her social potential.

We behave according to what we believe is true

As a nurse, I cared for a woman named Nadia who traveled from India to receive treatment in the United States. She had been diagnosed with lung cancer, and her husband wanted her to be cared for in this country. By the time arrangements could be made for the trip, Nadia had knowledge of her diagnosis for four weeks. Prior to her diagnosis, this woman felt perfectly well.

Following her diagnosis, Nadia began to lose weight, had aches and pains and felt weak. As it turned out, her x-ray had been misread, and there was absolutely no evidence of cancer at all. Living with the belief that she had cancer, Nadia experienced the very symptoms of the disease.

When an individual believes something is true, the body actually responds as though it is. The notion of the placebo effect illustrates the power of the mind over the body. When a doctor suggests that a specific pill will cause his patient to feel better, in many cases the patient improves even though the medicine contains only sugar with no medicinal value. Again and again we witness the power that the mind has on behavior. We behave and feel according to how our mind thinks things are and not necessarily in accordance with the way they are in fact.

A negative opinion of yourself

Psychologist Eugene Sagan coined the term pathological critic. The term refers to the negative inner voice that judges you. What happens is this:

Your mother tells you, on an on-going basis, that because you are shy you do not behave appropriately in social situations. She may not use these precise words, but the message is unmistakable. At some point you are labeled shy. Along with the shy word, you receive other terms and gestures that let you know that you are not okay.

After hearing them often enough, your mother's words become ingrained in your brain, creating your very own pathological critic. Each and every time that you are thrust into a social situation, your pathological critic reminds you that you are shy, and you are quite likely to behave in a shy manner. These negative thoughts keep you shy, and each failed social attempt shows you that your critical voice is correct.

Never create a pathological critic in your child

The way in which your child comes to see herself forms the foundation of her entire personality. Because of one basic belief, your child will actually tend to recreate the same scenario as hard as she may want to fight it, and each time her sense of a shy self will be reinforced. As time goes on, with repeated scenes of the same shy type behavior, your child has "proven" to herself that, yes, in fact, she is shy.

Consider how differently a child would feel, depending upon the outcome of this situation:

Jonathan is four years old and is clinging to his mother at a birthday party. It appears that all of the other children are having fun, yet Jonathan does not want to sit at the birthday table. He's put on the birthday hat, but he insists on sitting right next to his mother on an adjoining chair.

Scenario Number One

Jonathan's mother is embarrassed. This is the fourth birthday party where Jon has behaved this way and she is at her wits end. "That's it," she exclaims. "Either you sit down at the table right now or we are leaving."

Ten minutes later this extremely distraught mother is dragging a kicking and screaming Jonathan towards the door. Mom is humiliated, and Jon feels overwhelmed and sad. He knows that mommy is disappointed in him, and he feels ashamed. Jonathan is aware that he has behaved badly, but he is not really certain what he did wrong. "Why can't you just sit and have fun like the other kids? You are always so shy!" Mom declares.

After a few more episodes like this, Jon is very sure of four things:

1-He *is* shy.

2-Shy is *not* a good thing.

3-He feels ashamed of himself.

4-His unacceptable behavior will continue because he doesn't know how else to behave.

We are left with a very confused child who knows that what he is doing is not appropriate but has not been directed as to another way to behave. Jonathan is given the choice to either sit with the others and have fun, or leave. But because Jonathan does not have the ability to join in, he leaves the party more damaged than before.

Scenario Number Two

Jonathan's mother knows that her son feels clingy at parties. She sits on a chair and allows Jonathan to scrunch up next to her. When another mother asks, "What's wrong, is he shy?" Jon's mother replies in a very matter- of-fact way, "Oh no, he's not shy. Jon needs a little time to get used to parties just like I did as a kid. He'll sit at the table when he's ready." Jonathan's mother notices that he has reached for the birthday hat and has put it on. Jon chooses not to eat or play the games. When the party is over, Jonathan's mother makes a point of saying, "you must be very proud of yourself today. You put the birthday hat on all by yourself. Maybe next time you'll want to sit at the table."

Jonathan leaves the party feeling good about himself. He knows that his mother understands and respects him. After all, she felt as he does at parties when she was his age. Jon is developing an understanding of himself. He is learning that he needs a little time to get used to parties, too. There are no negative connotations, no disappointed feelings, and no shy word. Jon is learning not to label himself but merely to identify how he feels in specific situations. Jon thinks to himself, "maybe I'll feel like sitting at the kids' table the next time."

A change in vocabulary changes the way your child perceives herself.

It is extremely important to be aware of how we communicate with our shy children because what we say to them has an enormous impact on the way they feel about themselves. Psychological studies repeatedly find that a child's self-esteem directly stems from parental input. We teach our children whether or not to like themselves. Through the voice of their parents, a child receives daily input as to the type of person that we feel she is capable of becoming. Parents help children decide whether they are capable or unable, friendly or unfriendly.

Children desperately want to please their parents. Remember that what you tell your child she is capable of doing, she will actually accomplish. If you let your child know every day and at every appropriate opportunity that she is capable of being friendly, self assured, and social and that you are behind her 100 percent, your child will gain confidence in her own ability. She will envision herself in that way. If, on the other hand, you label your child as shy and convey to her the message that you don't believe she can behave in a socially-skilled manner, then that is precisely the way she will continue to develop.

Do we draw attention to the fact that the same child has an unsightly mole on her face? Or do we attempt to help her discover other things about herself to focus on?

Think for a moment how you feel when you develop a pimple on your nose. Don't you tend to focus on this fact throughout the day, giving it much more attention than it warrants? In actuality, the pimple makes up a very small portion of who you are, and, theoretically, you know this is true. Yet here you are, a mature adult, concentrating on the fact that there is a pimple on your nose. Absurd, but true.

The blemish of shyness

Imagine for a moment the impact that the word shy has on a child. Just as you feel that the entire world is staring at your pimple, the child who has been labeled as shy feels that absolutely everyone (including herself) sees her as shy. When we label our child as shy, it is as though she is wearing the shy word across her face. Rather than being able to focus on her other hidden potentials, the child who is labeled as shy is constantly aware of her blemish of shyness. In fact, the label of shyness becomes the focal point of your child's atten-tion. I am shy. These words have a tremendous amount of power to affect your child's entire life. Whether or not your child comes to think of herself in this way has much to do with you and how you help her see herself.

The evil spell of shyness

Our use of the shyness label brings to mind the popular fairy tale *The Frog Prince*. If you have not read the story lately, be sure to read it and share its' message with anyone who doesn't believe that the shy label is destructive to a child's sense of self. This fairy tale offers wonderful insight into the world of the shy child.

A handsome prince finds himself under a witch's spell. Trapped inside the body of a frog, the prince is forced to live as one, waiting to be rescued. The characteristics of the prince are not seen, and all that is expressed are frog-like behaviors.

The same is true when our child is labeled as shy, for she is encased in a hard outer layer of shyness. Our wonderful little girl or boy waits day in and day out to be rescued by us. We must strive to avoid casting the shyness spell at all. But if it already has been cast, we must work to remove the spell as quickly as possible. If your child looks in the mirror and sees a shy child looking back, her potential is only that of shyness. When her reflection is of a comfortable social being, then endless possibilities exist.

Our words and beliefs have power upon the development of our child's full potential

Carl Rogers, a well-known psychotherapist, supports the idea that people come to believe that they are a certain way because someone tells them so. Mommy calls me shy, therefore I must be. Where is the motivation for this child to even attempt to change? After all, it has already been established that she is expected to be shy.

Be careful what you call me

A three year old named Joe was an extremely energetic and friendly child. He easily approached other children and often led his peers when it came to what game they would play. His father saw him as a born leader and proudly gave him the nickname "pusher." As the months progressed, everyone began to notice a tremendous change in Joe's behavior. Rather than acting in his usual gentle, yet persuasive manner, Joe took to pushing other children around. Oftentimes his peers would end up crying, and Joe was a less sought-after friend. As his undesirable behavior continued, Joe became known as a bully and was avoided by other children.

His parents were totally perplexed as to why his personality had changed. Why had their seemingly friendly, good-natured child suddenly become aggressive? Coming to no conclusion on their own, Joe's worried parents sought the assistance of a child psychologist. The answer came after a few sessions. Joe had accepted the label of "pusher" and began to behave in a way that was consistent with the word. Joe was acting out the behavior that he thought was expected of him. "If I'm called a pusher, it must mean that dad expects me to push," Joe reasoned, and so began his drastic change of behavior. When the nickname was dropped and his parents explained what was meant by the term, Joe's previous behavior returned.

Joe had misinterpreted what his father originally meant and had developed a behavioral repertoire that was consistent with what he erroneously thought was expected of him. What a powerful lesson can be learned from this story. When we label our child in any way, she comes to accept our words and behaves in that manner. Our child defines herself and behaves in the way that she feels we define her.

Alfred Adler, a famous psychologist, created the notion of the inferiority complex. He stressed that the way you respond as a parent, either positively or negatively, transforms the development of your child's personality. It follows that a shy child who is labeled and made to feel not good enough (inferior) cannot possibly develop to her full potential. The flip side shows us that a nurtured child who is made to feel just wonderful about herself, who learns how specific situations make her feel and how she can cope with these feelings, is almost guaranteed to blossom.

Labeling is not accurate

On an ongoing basis, we label people with whom we come into contact. "She's so bossy," "he's so stubborn," "she's so shy." It has become common to pin labels on people we barely know. Yet when we put labels on people, we are generalizing and see that person in only one way. Our assessment is inaccurate because people rarely behave in a consistent manner.

Study this scenario because it illustrates a vital point:

Shy Melanie goes with her parents to visit Aunt Harriet. Aunt Harriet lives two hours away, and Melanie rarely gets to see her. During the visit Melanie nibbles on some cookies, says "thank you" when she is given milk, and smiles when Aunt Harriet talks to her. Melanie pulls away when Aunt Harriet goes to hug her, and she doesn't answer when she is asked about school.

As soon as Melanie begins to behave in ways that her parents deem to be shy, the intensity in the room starts to build. Now Melanie is being told to "stop acting shy," and the interaction between parents and child becomes negative. What does Melanie remember following the visit with Aunt Harriet? Does she recall the warm moments when she interacted very nicely, or the highly-charged negative interaction? More than likely, this child will not even be aware that she did a good number of things that warranted positive mention. Instead, she will come away from this visit feeling quite incompetent and more shy than before.

What we come to expect

When you label your child as shy, you tend to only see shy behavior. Shy is what you expect of her, and you are less likely to take note of the times your child is not shy. If you have any doubt that this is the case, think of an individual who you have labeled in another manner. Do you, for example, feel that someone you know is selfish? Have you ever noticed that all you see is how this person behaves in a selfish way? There she goes again, you think, as she proves to you, once again, how selfish she can be.

Could it be that sometimes she is generous, but you fail to take note of her generosity because you do not expect her to behave in this way? Do you really think that she is always selfish? That is unlikely. Similarly it is unlikely that your child is always shy.

Labeling is not only detrimental, but it is inaccurate for we are not predictable creatures (thankfully). We are easily influenced by the circumstances in which we find ourselves. Furthermore, and perhaps most encouraging, is the fact that we can change. Nothing about personality is an absolute. Each one of us is a tremendous storehouse of possibilities. What an exciting realization for our children and ourselves!

People do not behave in a consistent manner

An individual's behavior depends upon the place as well as the people who are involved in the encounter. Give it some thought and you realize that your child may be selfish at home but generous with friends, and shy with adults yet silly with children. Is she selfish and shy or generous and outgoing? The answer is not so simple because, depending upon the situation, we all behave in a variety of ways. Shy is an inaccurate term, for a child can behave both shy and outgoing, depending upon the situation. It is our job as a parent to help our child foster a belief that she can behave in a social manner, and then recognize the times she does so.

It appears to be magic when the social potential of a previously shy individual emerges. It looks as though new characteristics are developing, but, in reality, these abilities were always there. Potential abilities come forth when there is a belief that they exist in the first place. Arm your child with a belief system that is chock full of what she can do, and your child will be rewarded with a lifetime of strong abilities.

A shy child's thoughts prevent social behavior

Always remember that beliefs are only thoughts that may or may not be true. It is a fact that if a particular belief exists today, it does not have to exist tomorrow, for a change in beliefs leads to a change of thoughts and eventually a change in behavior.

I remember the day I was told that at times most people have felt self conscious at a party. What a revelation! I had been raised with the belief that everyone had a wonderful time at parties, and they always felt comfortable and at ease. Given this thought process, I had come to the unfortunate conclusion that something was clearly wrong with me. Once I learned I was not alone with my feelings, I changed my belief to a more realistic one. For the first time in my life, I no longer believed that I was the only one who felt uptight in such a situation. I was able to focus on the possibility that I could become more comfortable. I began to relax and eventually felt more socially at ease. As I changed my thoughts, I was able to change my behavior.

You will learn how to arm your child with the ability to put herself into social situations and succeed because her thoughts will dictate appropriate behaviors. Your child will come to believe in herself by developing a strong I CAN social belief system.

Your younger child will learn right from the start that she is capable. For the older child whose initial concept of herself is one of shyness, my program will lead your child to her own conclusion that her previously held shy beliefs were inaccurate and that she is capable of much more. The picture your child had for herself will slowly change, and her new system of beliefs will allow her to take on the role of potentially social. She will no longer have any use for her previous shy role. With your support, your child's perception of herself as having the ability to behave in a socially comfortable manner will grow very strong.

CHAPTER SEVEN

CREATING SOCIAL ABILITY

Help your child see herself as having the ability to be social and you will be surprised at how many times and in how many situations your child forgets to be shy.

The meaning of social

To be social implies some sort of ability to interact with others. For each person, the ability as well as the need is different. Some people desire constant interaction while others require a great deal of time by themselves. Neither approach is right or wrong, or more desirable than the other.

What specific behaviors enable a child to interact with her peers?

The process where a child acquires skills so that she is able to appropriately interact with her peers is referred to as socialization. Here we will refer to this ability as good friend-making behavior or GFM behavior. It is a fact that being a good friend, or being in possession of GFM behaviors has a lot to do with how your child is able to make the other person feel. In order to be successful in the social arena your child must learn to incorporate very specific GFM behaviors into each and every social situation in which she finds herself.

Babies naturally seem to know what to do

It is fascinating to note that babies appear to be pre-programmed with the initial skills necessary to begin to develop GFM behaviors. Babies will maintain eye contact at a very early age and will focus longer on a picture of a face where the eyes, nose, and mouth are placed in the correct positions than on one where the features are jumbled. Babies will turn in the direction of a voice and after a few months are sure to delight us with their smile.

Parents give tremendous amounts of positive attention to our baby's social behavior. We make it very clear with our words and gestures that smiling, eye contact, and reaching out are very much desired. Once baby begins eliciting GFM behaviors, it is likely that the behavior will be repeated often as baby takes delight in gaining positive responses from us.

The birth of the shy label

Jill, age three, does not tend to smile or speak very much in the presence of adults besides her parents. Her mother labels such behavior as shy and Jill frequently hears her saying "Jill is so shy." Jill's mother implies, by the tone of her voice and her body language, that shyness is a characteristic that she does not particularly favor.

Jill really does not know what shy means, but she is absolutely sure that being shy is not something to be proud of. Jill figures that there is a connection between when she doesn't feel ready to talk and being shy, and she worries about being in situations where her mother is likely to use the shy word again.

Pretty soon three-year-old Jill is not feeling very good about her ability to talk to others. The damaging effects of the shyness label have been set in motion, for Jill's self-esteem begins to suffer. Jill knows that she is a disappointment to mommy, and she begins to feel disappointed in herself. The most personally destructive aspect of this process is that Jill will become acutely aware of each occasion she fulfills her shy label. This innocent child has been thrown into a pattern that perpetuates her shy behavior, with a long list of negative feelings that become attached.

Shyness becomes a constant issue in such a household without much recognition of the good things that make up Jill's unique personality. What is not routinely noted is the fact that Jill is a rather pleasant little girl who is very gentle and kind to animals. She is good at painting and is beginning to read. All of these gifts that make Jill special become overshadowed by her shyness. Mommy rarely takes note of all of Jill's wonderful assets because she is consumed with how Jill will behave next. Shy, shy, shy. Jill hears the term so often that when she looks at herself, she sees only shy.

Bullied by shyness

When we view a child as shy, we lose sight of the complexity of the individual. By focusing on one small part of our child, we see only that part. Ask yourself what the typical behavior of a bully is. The bully threatens, she takes away power, and she creates worry and fear in the victim. "I know that the bully will bother me on the way home from school," a child worries. Just as the bully at school makes her victim feel awkward and unsure, the shyness bully rears its ugly head every time the child is faced with a challenging social situation.

"How else can I possibly behave?" the child questions, for the term has become the way that the child has been taught by us to define herself. There is no reason for her to expect to behave any other way because she knows that she is shy.

Every child has a right to feel safe from bullying

What gives us the right to use the shy word when we refer to our child? By addressing an individual in such a way, we are telling her, in no uncertain terms, that she does not measure up. Here lies the damage because even very young children know that it is not a good thing to be shy. No child should ever be labeled as shy. When we do so, we introduce our child to a way of thinking about herself that makes her the victim. Our child carries this self-defeating label into every social encounter that she faces.

Reconsider the case of Jill, using a healthier approach

Jill, age three, tends to be rather quiet and does not speak around adults other than her parents. Her mother has decided not to label her behavior but to specifically refer to Jill's actions. Jill's mother is also aware of how words and gestures affect her developing child, so she makes an extra effort to be aware of how she comes across. Jill's mother speaks calmly to her daughter.

"Jill, I know that you need a little while to get used to this new lady. I used to be the same way when I was your age. Do you want to sit with me, and you can say hello when you are ready?" Jill's mother gives her child a smile and a little wink and goes on with what she is doing. There is no negative body language, no sense of disappointment, and no shy label.

Jill knows that her mother understands her behavior around adults and that her feelings are respected. Jill is learning to understand herself with the implied expectation that she will feel comfortable enough to say hello eventually. It really doesn't matter if Jill succeeds during this particular social encounter or if she does not. Positive groundwork has been laid for the development of good friend-making behavior in the future.

Our most important job as parents

Of all the jobs we perform as parents, none rates quite as high as helping our child develop a feeling of positive self-esteem. Self-esteem is really a measure of how well your child likes or admires herself. It is directly related to how proud your child feels of who she is and what she is able to do. If your child genuinely feels that she is okay, then self-esteem will prevail. Your child must develop an "I believe I CAN" attitude in social situations. This "I CAN" attitude prepares your child to take on life's social interactions with the underlying belief that she is capable of success. This mind-set is fundamental to how close your child will come to reaching her social potential.

Acquiring high self-esteem

A child who develops high self-esteem accepts herself and her feelings as being okay. This does not mean she is unaware of her shortcomings, but rather and more important, that she recognizes those weaknesses and loves herself anyway. A child with low self-esteem feels negatively about herself and tends to look for acceptance from outside. This child needs to hear that she is okay from others in order for her to feel okay about herself. It is easy to see how an individual with low self-esteem never feels truly okay because one can never get enough outside approval. Instead of developing her own feelings of "I'm okay," a person with low self-esteem looks to others for those feelings and probably never finds them.

A study in self-esteem

Gabby was playing outside at recess. She approached two other girls and started to follow them down the slide. "You can't play with us," one of the girls said. "Go away!" Gabby sulked away and spent the remainder of recess sitting on the grass collecting rocks. That night she reported to her mother, "Nobody wanted to play with me at school today. Kids don't like me."

Here is a case of a child who looks outside herself for her own self worth. When Gabby doesn't get a favorable response, she comes to the conclusion she must not be likable. The tendency will be for Gabby to make less and less social attempts. This will lead to few successful interactions, reinforcing the idea that nobody likes her after all. Children with this mind-set focus on any sign of rejection as one more example of how unsocial and unlikable they really are.

It is not uncommon for women in particular to continue this thought process throughout life, always trying to please others in order to be liked. And being liked lets the person with low self-esteem feel, at least for a while, that she is okay. This process is not only exhausting, but it assures the individual of a very disappointing life. The person constantly measures her own worth by the feedback that she receives from others. Certainly this is not the life any one of us has in mind for our child. When we foster the development of a strong sense of self worth during childhood, positive feelings follow the individual throughout her entire lifetime.

And now return to scenario two where Gabby is a child with high self-esteem. Faced with identical rejection, Gabby would likely come to the following conclusion: "Those two girls are not being nice to me, so I'm going to find someone else to play with."

A child in possession of high self-esteem would view the response of the other girls as *their* problem and not hers. Because Gabby already knows she is okay, she does not need to get constant approval from others to feel good. She already possesses good feelings about herself deep within.

A timetable for shyness

An informative study by researchers named Younger, Schwartzman, and Ledingham helps us understand how important timing is in the intervention of our shy child. A group of children who were evaluated as being shy by their teacher were followed from second through fifth grade. The goal was to find out how these children were seen by their classmates and how they viewed themselves.

How were shy children viewed by their peers?

Shy children of all ages were avoided by their peers and were seen as being less approachable than more outgoing children. As children get older they begin to form opinions of the behavior of others and by age ten shy children were not only avoided; they were viewed in a negative way.

How did shy children see themselves?

In the second grade, the shy students saw themselves as not having the ability to be social. By the fifth grade, this same group reported feeling depressed and lonely.

These findings are somewhat encouraging because we appear to have time to work with our shy children to help them feel and behave in a more socially comfortable manner. According to this study, our potentially social child has until age ten to perfect her GFM behaviors before being viewed negatively by herself and others. (On page 99 you will find helpful tips for the older child.)

On creating confidence

We parents exert a crucial role in the development of self-esteem in our child. If our child feels deep down that we approve of her and are proud of her genuine self, then she gets the message that she is okay. Our words, our actions, and the body language we direct toward our child has a profound impact on how our child comes to evaluate herself. The absolute key to the acquisition of self-esteem is the possession of an "I CAN DO IT" attitude. Feelings of inadequacy ("I CANNOT DO IT") bring on low self-esteem. Here is how we parents can intervene in a very meaningful way:

If your child carries with her a feeling that she is unable to do something, she is sure to enter new situations with decreased confidence. When you label your child as shy, you teach your child to blame shyness for her discomfort in a social situation, and you remove her power to change. Your label of shyness makes a statement to her that she just is shy, and you give her little chance to grow.

A child who is helped to grow confident about what she is capable will come to view new situations with an expectation of success. Even if she fails, the child who possesses this "I CAN" belief will go into the next situation and will be willing to try again. When we replace pressure with understanding, we remove the negative component of social situations. We open the door for our child to experience positive social interactions.

CHAPTER EIGHT

WORDS THAT CHANGE
SHY TO SOCIAL

How does it feel to be shy?

For each child, the shy word will mean something different, but for all shy children it represents a strong belief that there is something they cannot do. Over the years, I have spoken to hundreds of children who were labeled shy. What follows is a list of beliefs shy children shared about what being shy meant to them:

> "I cannot make friends."
> "I cannot speak to people."
> "I cannot answer in class."
> "People just don't like me."
> "I cannot do anything well."

Although the specifics vary, all children who view themselves as shy live with an "I CANNOT DO" belief system. Not one child I ever questioned viewed shyness as a desirable attribute. Possession of this "I cannot do" belief system goes against the development of a child's positive self-esteem. It is a vital parental responsibility to make sure that your child develops an "I CAN DO" approach to social development. The messages you deliver to your child have enormous power to either push her in the direction of shyness—or social comfort.

Study the two columns below. The first column contains statements that encourage your child to remain shy by fostering an "I cannot" social belief system.

The second column is your child's "can do" column and contains words that result in a mind-set where your child comes to believe that she has the ability to behave in a social manner. Column two is where you find the words to support your child in a realistic yet loving manner, always with the expectation that social comfort is in her future.

Consistent use of statements from column two help your child understand her own behavior without being labeled in any way. Take note of the fact that the shy word is never used in the second column.

Column One	Column Two
What parents say to create an "I CANNOT" belief in their child	What parents say to create an "I CAN" belief in their child
"Why are you so shy? Say hello!"	"You need a little time to get used to new situations, and that's okay."
"Say something. Don't you have anything to say?"	"You have a lot to say. Take your time and join in when you feel ready."

"Look, everyone is talking and having a good time except you."

"Everyone feels unsure about what to say sometimes, and it's okay to feel that way."

"Stop being so shy. You look so uncomfortable. People will think you don't like them."

"Nobody can tell how you feel inside. Chances are others feel uncomfortable, too. You are not alone."

"Go have fun. Play with the kids. Don't be so shy."

"You need a little time to get used to parties or groups of people. Sit next to me until you feel ready to join in."

"Speak up. Nobody can hear you. Stop acting so shy."

"You are a soft spoken person. Some people speak with a low tone of voice. I did, too, when I was your age. As I got older, I felt ready to speak louder."

"Your teacher says that you don't raise your hand and don't talk enough in class. Stop being so shy."

"You will be able to talk in school when you are ready. I noticed that yesterday you smiled at the teacher. I am proud of you."

"Why are you always so shy? Why can't you be friendly?"

"Everyone feels uncomfortable sometimes. I used to feel that way, too. Remember the time you were friendly to the...."

"Don't you have anything interesting to say?"

"Everyone has times when they don't know what to say. Next time you can take a list to help you remember."

"Play the piano for grandpa and stop being so shy. This is your grandfather. Why are you acting this way?"	"You let us know if you feel ready to play the piano for our guests. Playing for others is not easy and is a brave thing to do."
"You're always so shy with everyone."	With a big smile you proudly declare, "Oh she's not shy. She needs time to get used to a party. She's just like I was at her age. She'll join in when she's ready."

When you view these columns side by side, it becomes crystal clear why we must adopt the second group of responses. By utilizing a precise, well thought out approach, we encourage our child to develop her social abilities in a nonthreatening atmosphere filled with love, support, and acceptance. We must always remember that the message we deliver to our child has the power to either encourage or discourage shy or socially comfortable behavior. To a great extent, the choice is ours. Let the second column guide your behavior, and what you previously thought was impossible for your child will become a reality – one patient step at a time.

CHAPTER NINE

CREATING A MIND-SET
FOR SOCIAL COMFORT

We parents, in the name of love, tend to protect our children as much as we can from the pain of living. We attempt to create an environment for our child that is as stress free as possible. By doing so, we teach our child that distress is to be avoided at all cost. In our effort to create the happiest childhood for our child, we shield her from the normal expected anxiety and stress of life. It is, however, only while experiencing a certain level of anxiety that any of us succeed.

I am an avid swimmer. In my attempt to teach Becky to swim, I came upon an interesting phenomenon. Although Becky knew the strokes and was able to swim in the shallow water, when I took her into the deep area she appeared to have forgotten how to stay afloat. Of course she had not really forgotten, but she did not feel safe. I encouraged her and explained that I understood that she was afraid, but she should push herself and try anyway. With time and encouragement, Becky swam comfortably in the deep water. Becky learned that she could experience anxiety, make mistakes, and still succeed.

Even though it does not feel good at the time, some anxiety helps us all attain our greatest accomplishments. Consider toddlers learning to walk. First they hold on gingerly to everything they can grasp, groping and hoisting themselves along. They may crash to the floor many times, only to be rescued and further encouraged by us. Certainly these little ones must feel anxious and unsure, but they have our support. Within this nurturing environment, toddlers continue to make mistakes in footing and balance. Yet one thing is for sure: in the end, after all the mistakes have been made, the child will walk.

Throughout childhood, every youngster conquers a multitude of fears and discomforts. Dark rooms begin to feel a lot more comfortable when a night-light is used. Visits to the doctor and dentist, with all the accompanying pokes and jabs, are a bit unnerving. Children learn to cope with uncomfortable feelings because they know that these encounters are absolutely necessary in order to remain strong and healthy.

Not only do most children deal with what is expected, but we parents fully expect them to cope. We would never think of our child as not being able to learn to use the bathroom, put on a coat, or ride the school bus. If we had such low expectations for our children, we would create a generation of helpless adults. Yet we think nothing of telling our child she is shy, hence unable to perform socially. We must expect that our shy child can be social.

Every time a shy child avoids a social situation because she believes that she can't handle it, a little piece of her positive self worth is chipped away and she feels disappointed in herself. It is always better for a child to at least make an attempt, and fail, than not try at all. If a shy child never tries to behave in a social manner because it is assumed that she cannot, then she will never really know how well she might have succeeded. She is left wondering how social she could have become. In this context, her social potential cannot be realized.

Parenting the fearful child

Children will sometimes express a fear of something you as a parent wish were not true. Particularly in the case of your shy child, you hear expressions of nervousness with regard to activities or occasions you hoped were fun for your child. Because these feelings are actually painful for us to hear, we have a tendency to dismiss them. "There's nothing to be afraid of," you assure her. "You should have fun at a party." By responding in this manner, you are telling your child her feelings are not real and the way she feels is inappropriate. An attempt to discard or judge our child's feelings will not make them go away, nor will this approach help our child learn how to handle her feelings any better. Instead, this type of interaction will encourage your child to keep more and more of her feelings to herself. When your child feels safe to express her anxieties and knows that you will be there to support her, no matter what, she will experience freedom to explore and develop the social potential that lies within.

An interesting study carried out by M. C. Jones shows how a specific parenting approach helps frightened children become more comfortable. A group of toddlers and their mothers were invited to enter a room in which there was a friendly looking clown. Some children were very happy to see the clown and walked right over to him while others pulled back or avoided any interaction with the clown at all.

The behavior of the frightened children was strongly influenced by the way their mother responded to them. When mothers failed to acknowledge their children's fears and pushed them to interact with the clown, the children became more upset. When mothers accepted their children's feelings and gave them support in a calm manner, the children tended to calm down and behave more comfortably. Some children even approached the clown.

When a child experiences anxiety about a particular situation, the parenting approach that has the greatest positive impact is the one where the parent is calm and supportive, not where the child is pushed to interact with the stressor. Children who are encouraged to take a risk at their own pace tend to do well. When we support our potentially social child and do not push her to do anything until she feels ready, the chance of her overall social success increases greatly.

It is normal to feel uncomfortable

It is important to educate our potentially social child. Help her realize that she may feel uncomfortable in specific social situations, but that she remains safe to attempt particular behaviors without the risk of criticism and ridicule from us. Isn't that what growing up is all about? It is the courage to try new things with the belief that we will be able to handle the challenges. Whether we succeed or fail, we make the attempt anyway.

Underlying this thought process is a system of beliefs that understands that the process may be downright frightening, but still we go ahead and try. When inevitable mistakes are made, we do not belittle ourselves for having made them. Instead, we give ourselves credit for having tried.

Chapter Ten

Expected to be Shy
or Learning to be Social

Parental attention and, more specifically, praise and recognition of a behavior, is a huge reward for a child. Whether or not a certain behavior is desired, when we draw attention to it the behavior will increase. Children want our attention any way they can get it. This means they will accept attention for the good they do, or they will take it for the bad. We must carefully pick the behaviors we want to encourage in our child because attention to a specific behavior serves as a reinforcement and literally guarantees that it will be repeated.

Past experiences either encourage or discourage future behavior. Teaching your child to wave is a perfect example. If your child waves to the neighbor and she gets a big smile and a wave back, your child has had a positive experience with her waving and is likely to wave again. But if people respond to your child's waving by looking away or with a grimace, she is less likely to continue her waving pursuits. When your child has had an experience at a friend's house where she felt socially uncomfortable, she is likely to become tense when confronted with that friend's invitation to visit the next time.

A very well-known study by J. B. Watson demonstrates this concept. An 11-month-old boy named Albert was shown a white rat, which he crawled towards with interest. This pattern was repeated many times. After a while, a loud noise was made by hitting a steel bar every time Albert began to approach the rat. As would be expected, Albert became frightened and began to cry. Following a few identical sequences, Albert cried and crawled away every time he saw the rat, whether or not the loud noise was made. Albert became fearful of the rat.

In the same way, if your child has a number of negative social experiences, she comes to associate social situations with discomfort. The negative comments, the pushing to join in, the labeling of shyness, all take the place of Albert's loud noise. As these negative experiences become ingrained in your child's mind, any social situation is associated with fear.

For some children, the mere mention of plans to attend a party brings forth a litany of negative emotions, even before they enter the car to drive there. Our child anticipates yet another uncomfortable social encounter. "Are you going to play this time?" "Go kiss Aunt Marla hello," we suggest. All of these well-meaning options delivered by the loving parents we are increase the stress and negative anticipation our child feels prior to the social event. And our child is not the only one who feels worried about facing a social encounter. Parents become anxious, too. Social interactions become an emotionally-charged ordeal for you and your child.

People generalize from one situation to another

If a situation has enough in common with the original one, people tend to react similarly. Eleven-month-old Albert came to fear furry white objects such as cotton balls, a fur coat, and a white bearded Santa Claus mask, even though he never had a bad experience with any of them. We can see how this phenomenon applies to our potentially social child when we label and denigrate her. Is it any wonder that she remains shy and may even appear to get worse? It certainly should come as no surprise that her shy behavior begins to involve more and more social situations. Yet there are things you can do to help your child look at social events in a positive way.

Reinforcement encourages desired behavior

A child psychologist by the name of Sidney Bijou conducted a study of praise and its effect on social behavior. He became aware of a nursery school child who was extremely withdrawn and did not interact with the other children. Following Bijou's advice, the teachers began to praise the child each time she made any move towards the other children. With time this little girl developed into an active member of her class.

Reinforcement is most effective when it is given immediately following a desired behavior. Manu-facturers of computer games know this, and the delivery of positive reinforcement is perfectly timed. When your child responds correctly, bells sound, music plays, and colors glow. Is it any wonder that your child plays her computer game over and over again?

When teachers use stars to reward good behavior, the child is reinforced in two ways. She gets positive reinforcement by earning a star as well as extra attention from the teacher. A positive response from the teacher lets the child know that her behavior is valuable. Because the teacher is on the lookout for good behavior, more attention is paid to what the child is doing right. When the teacher-student interaction becomes focused on the positive, the child comes to expects more of herself. (You will learn how to reward your child to help her perfect her GFM behaviors.)

Be careful not to reinforce the negative

It is a well known fact that teachers must be cautious not to overly correct children as they begin to read. If a new reader is corrected each time she mispronounces a word, she becomes flustered and tends to mispronounce even more. It is by the same mechanism that we correct our shy child's behavior with ongoing criticism. Some parents, in their quest to help their child function socially, reprimand and punish them for not being socially successful. When we do not include positive reinforcement for what she is doing well, we interfere with any learning that could possibly take place. As a direct result of our actions, we turn our child off to learning appropriate social skills.

Suppose your child is waiting to go into school. "Say hello to Suzy," you chide. "Oh look, there's Jane. Why don't you walk over to her?" To a potentially social child you may be asking her to do the impossible. Your child may well need time to observe the situation before she can act. "Say hello" and "walk over" are all ways we give our child attention for their shy behavior. Knowing that any form of attention actually reinforces behavior, we have reinforced our child's shy response. If we add the "stop being shy" jargon, we increase her discomfort around social situations, further increasing the chance that shy behavior will recur.

Positive reinforcement changes behavior

Praise and encouragement can really turn a situation around. When Becky was two, she was riding in a shopping cart exiting a supermarket. The door must have been faulty because it closed with a loud crash directly onto our cart. Becky screamed.

Following the incident, Becky would cry and hold onto me whenever she saw an automatic door. Becky was afraid of the door. For a period of six months, every time Becky would pass through such a doorway, even if I carried her, I praised her. Eventually she became comfortable riding in a shopping cart again. Positive reinforcement had changed Becky's behavior.

Attempt to recall the last time you gave your child a compliment for smiling at another child or standing in a group. We tend to ignore "good" behavior and point out and label the "bad." Remember, praise and reinforcement encourages desirable behavior.

When we heap complaint upon complaint each time our child finds herself in a social situation, she will learn to fear these situations without a clue as to how she could better succeed. In fact, her shy behavior will tend to increase.

When you are on your child's side during social endeavors, and you are careful to reinforce her for desirable behaviors, your child will increase her GFM behaviors. As your child becomes more and more successful in social situations, she will learn that she can succeed. Her personal successes then serve as their own positive reinforcers.

CHAPTER ELEVEN

CAN DO PARENTING

What would it have meant to you had your parents appreciated you for who you really were, with no labels, no negative judgments, and no feelings of disappointment?

Some of us had that experience, and some of us will never get this type of understanding from our parents. You have the opportunity to give this gift to your child.

What kind of parent am I?

This exercise will help you evaluate your parenting (and teaching) style. Carry out the following exercise for one week. At the end of the week, you will come to see the way in which you relate to your child. Each day ask yourself the following questions:

1. Do I withdraw my love when my child clings to me in a social situation?

2. Do I expect that my child will behave in a shy manner and do I label her?

3. Do I reinforce my child for being "nice and quiet?"

Determining your parenting style

As you keep track of the answers to these questions, you will come to see a pattern in your responses. Where do you fall?

I use BODY LANGUAGE

I roll my eyes, push my child away, or by other means let my child know that I am displeased by her behavior.

I use NEGATIVE WORDS

I voice various versions of the following statements of upset:

"Here you go again, sitting around. You're supposed to be having fun."
"Stop hanging on me!"
"Look, everyone else is having fun at the party."
"Why do I take you to parties if you never have any fun?"

I use LABELING

The shy word comes up frequently when I am referring to my child either directly or indirectly.

"Is she shy? Oh, yes!"
"You are acting so shy."
"Why do you always have to be so shy?"

I use REINFORCING BEHAVIOR

I make excuses for my child and use her shy behavior in
a positive encouraging way.
"She's just my shy little girl. Isn't she sweet?"
"She's shy – she doesn't want to play."
"You just love mommy. Here, come sit on my lap."

How do you relate to your child?

This may be the first time you have critically evaluated the way that you interact with your child. You may come away from this exercise feeling disappointed in yourself for behaving in a certain manner, and you may be ashamed at some of the things that you have done or said. Instead of feeling badly about yourself, use this awareness to change your behavior. When you are ready, turn to the next chapter and make a commitment to parent your child with words and actions that will bring out her social best.

CHAPTER TWELVE

A SILENT PLEDGE TO MY CHILD

What follows are the bricks and mortar to foster your child's social success. These beliefs are fundamental to the creation of an environment that encourages the social development of your child. Silently deliver this pledge to your child. The precise words need not be spoken, yet your actions from this point forth must be consistent with these vital thoughts.

I WILL HELP MY CHILD LEARN THAT...

If you feel unsure of yourself, other people do not know that you are feeling that way. Furthermore, it is possible that they feel uncertain, too.

The quiet side of you is wonderful. You are aware of your own feelings, which makes you sensitive to other people's feelings as well. These are characteristics of a good friend. Because of your sensitive nature, you choose friends carefully and wisely.

It is a good thing to connect with other people, but you may not need to be friends with everyone. It is special to have a few close friends. You make the choice as to what is comfortable for you.

You will make mistakes; everyone does, and that's okay. Always remember that when you learned to walk you fell. But you tried again and again, small steps each time, until you could do it. Just as you had to learn to walk before you ran, you may need to learn to simply walk into a room full of people before you will feel ready to join in.

I will never discipline you for your social attempts. I will not punish you or bring attention to the things that you do or do not do that may be socially inappropriate.

I will never compare you to other more socially comfortable children.

I will never say that you "should" do anything. What may seem right for me may not be right for you.

I will never label you as shy or in any other way, and I will not permit others to do so. Labeling is disrespectful and does not allow us to see the real person behind the label.

I will tell you daily at least one thing that makes you wonderful. As you listen to my positive words, you will come to speak to yourself in the very same way.

I will help you to dispel your shyness inventory. Rather than ever use the shyness word to identify any of your behavior, I will address each situation in very specific terms. "You need time to look around first before you feel ready to play."

I will help you put your feelings into words. When you require my help in a social situation, I will support you in such a way that you feel comfortable asking for what you need.

I will help you learn how to be a good friend. With my own words and behaviors, I will show you how compliments and becoming a good listener can make you a very desirable friend. I will become a good friend to you. I will show a genuine interest in what you do and say, and I will look directly into your eyes to make a strong connection.

I will speak with your teachers, baby-sitters, and relatives to be sure that all individuals who are in contact with you utilize the same approach and respond to you with a positive, non-labeling approach.

Every day I will show you
an appreciation for who you are
and a belief in what you can become.

CHAPTER THIRTEEN

PULLING IT ALL TOGETHER:
A FORMULA FOR SOCIAL SUCCESS

Bringing out the best in a potentially social child requires a very specific set of adult-centered guidelines plus an organized way for the child to approach each and every social encounter. Adults need to master the You CAN DO IT Parent Support Program while the child must perfect the READY, SET, GO Social Readiness Program. At first each step must be performed quite intentionally. Once mastered, every social encounter will be approached in the same fashion, giving you and your child a formula for social success.

•••••

You CAN DO IT Parent Support Program

Systematically go through each step whenever you and your child are in a social situation. With time the steps will become habit, and you will not even think about what to do next.

Realize the power you have as a parent. How you speak to your child and the feedback you provide has a direct effect upon the development of your child's social potential. Remind yourself of the pledge you silently delivered to your child.

You CAN DO IT
Parent Support Program
1. Count
2. Assess
3. No negative comments
4. Describe child's behavior
5. Okay like mom and dad
6. Initiate or observe a social gesture
7. Time reinforcement during social event
8. Final proud statement after social event
9. End with potential for further social growth

Step 1: Count

How? Silently count to ten.

Why? Gives adult an opportunity to evaluate the social atmosphere and pause before becoming involved.

Step 2: Assess

How? Assess the type of behavior your child is displaying and be on the lookout for opportunities for her to become involved in the social situation in any way.

Why? Allows you to set up opportunities for child to experience social success. Think of any way your child can involve herself, even minimally, in the social situation.

Step 3: No negative comments

How? Say nothing negative to your child about what she is or is not doing.

Why? Allows child to be part of a social encounter without any negative feedback from you.

Step 4: Describe child's behavior

How? Give a short positive statement that specifically describes her actions. Include comments that set the stage for future good social behavior. "You need time to get used to this party. If you would like, you can stay with me until you feel ready to sit at the table."

Do not show negative response or disappointment. Be aware of your tone of voice, your body language, and your words. Do not label and do not allow others to do so either. Negate any label that is directed at your child, and describe the situation for the other person. "Oh no, she's not shy. She needs time to get used to the party. She'll stay here until she feels ready to sit down."

Why? Encourages your child to feel good about how she is behaving. The idea is to clarify for her that you understand her needs and are supportive without pressure. It is she who decides when to make the next move. Rather than have your child feel "I'm not good enough...I CAN'T," your words and actions help your child develop a vocabulary of success-strength-ening terms such as, "I'm waiting a while and then I'll be ready to say hello." When you help your child learn how to approach social situations with a feeling of power, her behavior changes from "I CAN'T because I am shy," to "I CAN be social when I am ready." Give your child the belief in herself that she CAN succeed socially, and she will.

Step 5: Okay like mom and dad

How? Make a statement such as "I needed time to get used to parties when I was your age, but after a while I was ready to walk right in."

Why? All children want to identify with their parent. A statement such as this reinforces the feeling that they are okay and just like mom or dad was at their age. There is not a child who does not like to hear how much they look like mommy or daddy, or how they throw a ball or can climb as well as their parent. Identification with a parent is an exceptionally strong positive learning tool. (If reference to a parent does not apply, identification with a relative or friend is also effective.)

Step 6: Initiate or observe a social gesture

How? During the social encounter, observe your child for the smallest social gesture, even if you have sug-gested it.

Why? We are only able to reinforce a specific behavior that has occurred. Therefore, it may be necessary for you to create a situation where a desired behavior is acted out by your child so that you may offer praise and encouragement. For example, suggest to your child that she perform a small task such as walking into the party room without holding your hand, and reinforce that action later. Be careful about the frequency and the means by which you praise your child. Most potentially social children feel uncomfortable when praise is delivered in an overly exuberant manner. Make sure you are aware of the type of reinforcement that is most meaningful to your child. Avoid constantly reinforcing your child for every move she makes. Constant feedback will turn your child off to praise in general and will water down the effectiveness when it is appropriately given.

Step 7: Time reinforcement during social event

How? Whatever gesture is used (thumb up, smile, hug), quickly reinforce your child at the exact moment that the desired social act is performed. Make sure that you offer reinforcement for a specific behavior and avoid generalities such as "You did well."

Why? It is highly effective for your child to hear what exactly she has done that is so desirable. "Good singing," lets your child know specifically what she did that was praiseworthy. She will be more likely to repeat her behavior the next time a similar opportunity presents itself.

Step 8: Final proud statement after social event

How? Upon leaving the social situation, quietly comment to your child how proud you are of her specific behavior, and suggest that she must be proud of herself. "I am so proud of you for reaching for the cup," or "You must be so proud of yourself that..."

Why? The goal is to equip your child with reinforcing language so that she will develop a positive self praise system for herself. With time you will know you have accomplished your goal when your child comes to you and says, "Mommy, I was so proud of myself when I..." At this moment your child has made the monumental step of internalizing your positive statements, making them her own personal talk.

Step 9: End with potential for further social growth

How? Leave off with "maybe sometime soon or next time when you are ready you will want to...take it a step further." Leave it as the child's decision, not yours. Give the power to your child.

Why? This type of statement will give your child a feeling of control over future social endeavors. By delivering a quick, non-pressure statement, you are giving your child the decision-making responsibility for her own social behavior. Your child will come away from each social event with a wonderful feeling. "I CAN do it by myself and according to my own personal time frame. I decide when." You have given the power to your child. She is free to decide how she wishes to behave and when she will be ready to do so.

• • • • • •

READY, SET, GO Social Readiness Program
for the Potentially Social Child

This step-by-step program will help your child maximize her potential to be social and must be carried out every time your child is in a social situation. The program is designed so that in between each challenging step your child is given the chance to pause, giving her the impetus to continue.

Help your child realize that the process of social growth consists of both challenges and fun. You will need to go over each step with your child until she has memorized them all. Refer to the song at the end of this chapter to help your child remember what she needs to do. Role play with your child at home so that she will become comfortable enough with the steps to be willing to try them out in public.

As you help your child develop a repertoire of behaviors incorporating the tools she needs to succeed socially, your child will begin to see herself in a way that is compatible with being social. Instead of focusing on the negative and what your child is NOT doing, you will be giving positive attention for that which your child CAN do. You will relish in your child's small accomplishments, and you will feel pride for your child that you have never felt before. The thrust of your interactions with your child will change from negative criticism to positive praise.

You will see your child for the way she really is

Extremely important to the growth of your child is the fact that you will begin to see her more realistically. Instead of instructing your potentially social child to "go play and stop being shy," you are introducing a plan of action to help her manage herself within her social environment. When you change your expectations for your child from something that is so final (she's just shy) to something that is realistically hopeful (increasing her GFM behaviors), then all kinds of exciting social responses begin to emerge. As your child puts forth GFM behaviors, she will experience positive feedback directly from the situation, from you, and, most important, from herself.

You will help your child establish a strong social belief system, while, at the same time teaching and encouraging her to be comfortable with her GFM behavioral repertoire. With time, your child will develop the ability to systematically choose appropriate behaviors from her GFM action list. Your child will be able to bring to mind a list of CAN DO social behaviors. Feel free to add or remove any items so that you tailor this list to the specific needs and style of your child.

GFM Action List

Smile

Look into other person's eyes

Eat

Sit down with others

Play

Ask questions

Your child will develop a new way of looking at herself

When your child begins to realize that she CAN choose social behaviors, brand new positive feelings about herself emerge. "I am shy," is confidently replaced by "I CAN be social." Instead of feeling that she is all of those negative characteristics associated with being shy, your child will learn to identify herself with more desirable characteristics. She is likely to discard the characteristics from the first column and replace them with social attributes from the second column below. As she does so, you will witness the birth of your social child.

SHY	SOCIAL
Boring	Interesting
Not well liked	Likeable
CAN'T be a good friend	CAN be a good friend

When you help your child develop a set of positive, encouraging thoughts about herself, instead of negative, self-defeating ones, the change in her attitude is remarkable. Your child begins to believe in herself. She will firmly conclude that she has the knowledge and ability to behave in a social manner. Suddenly your child has an endless future of wonderful social adventures.

For the older child

Your child, depending on her age, has repeatedly responded to social situations in a shy manner. Her destructive thoughts have gotten in the way of more favorable responses. The READY, SET, GO Program incorporates positive self talk, moving your child forward one step at a time.

Rather than allow the free flow of negative thoughts and ideas, your child will learn to replace these with more meaningful and valuable self-guidance techniques. She will learn to put these steps into practice whenever a social encounter arises. Your child will be in charge of her thoughts, and eventually in charge of every social encounter in which she engages.

It is quite probable, particularly with the older child who has had a longer history of a negative thought pattern, that at the initiation of the program, your child will hold onto negative thoughts and labels because she has become so used to them. Discuss this with your child and let her know this is to be expected. After all, you are breaking a deeply enmeshed habit. Stress to her that thoughts CAN change. Let her be aware of her negative self talk and have her practice substituting new beliefs for the old, familiar words.

> I am shy.
>
> I can't talk in front of a group of people.
>
> I'm different from everyone else.

CAN become

> I'm not shy.
>
> I will talk when I'm ready. I just need to take my time.
>
> Everyone feels uncomfortable at certain times,
>
> and I am not the only one.

For adults who are shy

The READY, SET, GO Social Readiness Program can be fine-tuned for shy adults. As is true of the older shy child, you have had a lifetime of social situations in which you behaved in a shy manner. Shy behavior is how you identify yourself.

The READY, SET, GO Program will get you in the habit of step-by-step thinking each and every time you find yourself in a social situation. With practice, the steps will become automatic, and you will no longer have to think about what to do next. Follow the suggestions for the older shy child and pay particularly close attention to the words you use when you speak to yourself.

When you change your thoughts, you will change your behavior. As you experience social success, you will gain the confidence to place yourself into more and more social encounters.

READY, SET, GO Social Readiness Program

Countdown

READY

Happy Thought

SET

I CAN do my best

GO

Reward

Good try!

Tomorrow is another day

Step 1: Countdown

How? Pause and take a deep breath and count down ten to one.

Why? Allows child to get her bearings and relax before she begins.

Step 2: READY

How? Child will look around and think of the ways in which she is able to behave in a social manner.

Why? Your child must think of herself as having the ability to behave in a social manner. This goal is natural when you do not label your child as shy. Rather than think of herself as shy, with all of the things she can't do, your child comes to believe that there are many things that she CAN do. If your child believes she has the ability to be social, then she will be social.

Step 3: Happy Thought

How? Child will take a moment and think of something that makes her happy. Whether it is a stuffed animal, a funny story, or a place she loves to go, your child thinks of something that gives her pleasure and does not allow anxious thoughts to prevent her from acting.

Why? It is important that your child learn to cope with feelings of anxiety, which are likely to surface as she is placed in a variety of social situations. Teach your child that these feelings are normal and are experienced by everyone. She must come to realize that she is capable of dealing with discomfort. Happy thoughts will encourage her to continue, knowing that she will be okay.

Step 4: SET

How? Child will picture in her mind what she will do, where she will go, what she might say, and how she will say it. Child may choose from her GFM action list or figure out another way she would like to participate.

Why? By picturing herself behaving in a social manner, your child learns to think before she acts. Visualizing herself as having social ability helps her believe in herself and perfect her actions.

Step 5: I CAN do my best

How? Child will tell herself that she will do her best.

Why? With your supportive input, your child believes that she CAN behave in a social manner and all she has to do is try her best.

Step 6: GO

How? Child will do whatever she decided to do from her GFM behavior list.

Why? Child makes her own decision about how to behave.

Step 7: Reward

How? Child will reward herself. Discuss with your

child whether a reward at that very moment would be more fun or if a reward later on would be more desired. Becky sometimes chose to carry stickers or a small piece of candy with which she rewarded herself after performing a GFM behavior. Although rewards are most effective when they immediately follow the desired behavior, sometimes Becky chose to wait until later so that she could look forward to something at home. The anticipation was the reward itself. Encourage your child to cater her reward system to whatever approach she prefers.

Why? Self reward is a successful way to change behavior. As it becomes routine for the child to reinforce herself, she will be more likely to continue her desired social behaviors in similar situations in the future. This action also encourages the child to appreciate her own efforts. When a child learns to treasure herself and her efforts, she develops strong self-esteem.

Step 8: Good try!

How? Child gives herself credit for trying. Teach your child that giving up is not an option.

Why? Your child will learn that she can cope with her own anxiety, and she can push herself even if she would rather not do so. No matter what the end result is, she tried and lived through the experience. Your child will have learned a powerful lesson about her ability to cope. To try is always better than to do nothing, no matter how she does.

Step 9: Tomorrow is another day

How? Child tells herself that tomorrow is another day. The child must become familiar with the idea that even though her social goal may not have been reached today, tomorrow gives her another opportunity to succeed. She may not have behaved in a socially comfortable manner YET, but she will do so another day.

Why? The child is reminded of the inspiring word "yet." Even if she has not mastered her GFM behaviors and achieved social comfort today, she will have many more opportunities to improve her efforts.

Mastering the READY, SET, GO
Social Readiness Program is fun

A technique called mnemonics makes it much easier to remember lists. It is a proven fact that the use of a song helps individuals retain information. I used this approach with Becky when it was time for her to learn her social cues. Singing the words made it a fun experience to integrate the steps of the READY, SET, GO Social Readiness Program into Becky's mind. For hours on end, Becky would sing her Social Me song. During our first few outings following the introduction of the program, it was not unusual to hear Becky humming the familiar tune.

What follows is a sing song approach to help your child remember what it is that she must do every time she finds herself in a social situation. Teach your child the song and work with her to help her incorporate a strong belief in her own social abilities. After a while, these steps will become a natural part of her social behavior and she will perform them automatically.

READY, SET, GO Social Me Song
(sung to the tune of Yankee Doodle)

Wait and take a deep long breath
And count down 10 to 1

Look around and get ready
So I CAN be a social me.

Tell myself I'll do my best
And think of something happy.

Imagine how I'll thank myself
And READY, SET, and GO my way.

I know that I may feel scared
But I will do it anyway.

If I don't do so well
It really is okay.

I know that I have tried my best
And tomorrow is another day.

I'm so proud of myself, you see,
'cause I CAN be a social me!

©Laurie Adelman, 2007

Chapter Fourteen

Social Skill Builders

Once you have mastered the You CAN DO IT Parent Support Program and your child has a feel for the READY, SET, GO Social Readiness Program, you will want to introduce some of the following techniques to further encourage your child to practice her new-found social skills. Read through these Social Skill Builders and select the ones that are geared to the particular needs of your child.

It is Brave to be Friendly

From this moment on, be aware of the fact that your child studies your every move. You are the primary model from which your child learns how to interact with her environment. Seize every opportunity to show your child what it is to be social. Here is your chance to demonstrate how GFM behaviors can become a natural part of everyday life. Let your child see you greeting neighbors and friends in a warm and friendly manner.

Routinely compliment others for the way that they dress or behave. When you are engaging in conversation with another individual, demonstrate behavior that encourages further conversation. Nod your head and say "yes" and "uh huh" and ask questions to move the conversation along.

Share your feelings as you demonstrate each behavior. Comments such as, "It was hard for me to say hello to our neighbor because I really don't know him, but now I feel so proud of myself because he was so nice" go a long way to show your child that even though a situation made you feel uncomfortable at first, your feeling of pride and the ability to make a new friend are well worth the initial anxious feelings. When you consistently share these feelings with your child, she will come to the wise conclusion that behaving in a social manner is a brave and desirable way to behave.

Imagine That

Your child is ready. You have worked with her for some time and the feeling around your home is one of support and acceptance. Your child has learned the READY, SET, GO Social Readiness Program and has demonstrated increasing expertise in carrying out her new-found skills. As luck would have it, your youngster has been invited to a classmate's birthday party; perfect timing to practice her new skills. As the day approaches, you see your child's enthusiasm waning. In place of her initial excitement, you observe signs of worry. In addition to offering support and understanding, there is a technique that works wonders when it comes to smoothing frayed nerves and helping your child back on the road to social success.

Nervous public speakers are advised to imagine the entire audience in their underwear. You can take this advice and customize it to the needs of your child. Depending upon her age, Becky imagined either one or an entire class of her peers in various forms of silliness. When she was very small, I told Becky to picture her audience with stuffed animals on their heads. Instead of speaking to a schoolmate, Becky was actually, at least initially, speaking to a stuffed Big Bird. Imagine my delight as I watched Becky smile as she spoke. She may have been entertained by her image of Big Bird, but as far as her audience was concerned, Becky appeared to be happy and at ease talking to them. Once she began to feel more comfortable, her imagined friends made less frequent appearances, by her request.

Customize this method to the needs of your child. Both of you can have a lot of fun thinking about the funny scenes that can be imagined. Not only is this a delightful stress breaker, but your child is indirectly reinforcing herself with a pleasant image as a result of carrying out a social gesture.

How Can I Play If I Don't Yet Know What to Say?

There is a fascinating bit of psychology involved in the making of play dates. It is a status symbol when a child is having a friend over to play. When Becky attended preschool and elementary school, a great deal of attention and excitement was spent on who was going home to play with whom after school that day. The children took great interest in the fine details of the arrangements that were made.

It is important for your child to become involved in this process as well. Not only does her involvement let her know that she is a desirable play date, but the child who is to come home with her to play will be attracted to her during the school day. A powerful bond exists between play date partners.

You may initially feel that your child is not ready for a play date because, after all, the idea is to play. What if your child is unlikely to utter one word? The answer lies in what I call the "somewhat silent play date." Let me assure you that Becky hosted many of these, each more successful than the first. There came a time when children were asking if they could come over to our house to play.

I realized that very little, if no, speaking would occur during the course of Becky's play dates, at least initially. I had to come up with a way to have the children interact a little and still come away from it having fun. I also wanted to create a situation where Becky would enjoy herself without any pressure to perform. The goal was to have Becky experience a successful play date so that she would want to have more.

It took some planning on my part, but the results were well worth my efforts. Before the child was scheduled to come to visit, Becky and I would discuss what we would plan to do. The worst scenario for a potentially social child is to have her in an open-ended situation where another child is merely coming over to play without direction.

Becky and I found that the act of baking worked extremely well. I found a recipe from scratch that contained a good number of steps. The children would sit down at the kitchen table and each child would take a turn performing a step. When we finished, which usually was at least 45 minutes to an hour, my kitchen table was a mess. Each child was given brushes and sponges to clean up the mess. We had many a giggle over who had flour on their nose or clothes. By the time we straightened up the area, the cookies or cake was done. Next came the most fun of all. I always had on hand a wide variety of colored frosting and sprinkles, and the children decorated their creations. By the time they were finished, the other child's mother was waiting to pick her up. We enjoyed a snack and the child went home. A wonderful time was had by all.

Following each play date, another phenomenon would occur. The next day at school the child would approach Becky and begin to talk about the fun they had. Not only did Becky feel the positive effects of friendship, but she became sought after. Play dates were fun after all.

Look What I Have for You: Helping Me Belong

When you are just beginning to work with your child on the development of her social skills, you search for a way to give your child a boost of self confidence without too much pressure. I discovered, by accident at first, a wonderful method for accomplishing this goal.

One day Becky and I were waiting outside her preschool classroom for the doors to open so that the children could walk inside. Most of the children were being quite boisterous and were holding hands and interacting in various ways. Becky was standing quietly by my side, not involved in the interactions going on around her. I had just come from the school store where I had purchased some snacks for later. Becky asked me if she could have one. When I complied, something wonderful happened. One by one, the children who had been playing came over to Becky and asked if they could have a snack. Becky's face lit up as she handed a snack to each child. "Thank you, Becky," was heard throughout the hallway. Even more spectacular was that a few of the children told Becky that they would bring some-thing special for her the next day. Before the doors of the classroom opened, Becky was invited to play with three children.

So what am I telling you? Do you carry around packages of food and let your child feed every kid with whom you come in contact? Not quite. Take the information from this incident and create important confidence-boosting events for your child. A child appears to possess an attractive force when she has something to share. As a matter of fact, we discovered that when Becky gave out papers during class or when she handed out crayons, a similar phenomenon occurred. Other children sought her out more and, by virtue of her being in control of the situation, this seemingly simple activity made her important in her own eyes as well as in the eyes of her peers. Throughout the years, I have suggested use of this technique to many of Becky's teachers. They all reported positive results.

We all have a need to belong. Yet it is common to find our potentially social child excluded from the main-stream. Potentially social children are often overlooked by other children because they have not yet learned how to interact. When a child feels she does not belong, she loses the incentive to make the attempt to participate. She has failed before she starts.

Remedy this unfortunate cycle of events by involving your child in any activity that requires her to be in charge. With time, you will see that this small action will build confidence while making her more visible and sought after. Teachers can be made aware of this technique, and it can easily be incorporated into the classroom as well as into social situations. Whenever we had company to our house, Becky handed out napkins, collected guest's coats, and passed out snacks. At first she did not utter a word as she dutifully carried out the deed, but as time went on and she became more confident, Becky was conversing beautifully. Put your child in control, and pretty soon she will feel in control of her ability to become social.

Add-One Game

When Becky was three, I created a game that continued for four years. Every day Becky and I each had to speak to one new person. It did not matter who that person was, only that we had never spoken to the individual before. At school Becky was free to choose who it was that she spoke to, but outside of school the rule was that she had to be with an adult to avoid a problem with strangers.

At the end of each day, Becky and I reported who we spoke to and how the discussion went. At the beginning of the game, we found that we enjoyed just reporting who we had spoken to that day. But as time went on, we felt that we wanted to keep track of how many new contacts we had made. One day an idea struck me, and it really caught on.

During the holidays we would often make decorations that consisted of a piece of paper, which was folded in four, drawn with people holding hands, and cut along the lines so that, once completed, we had a sequence of people holding hands. I thought, why not use the same idea and apply it to the new acquaintances we had made?

Becky and I each created a people chain. Every evening we would add one or more people to the lineup. You can imagine how long our chain became at the end of four years. Not only was this a fun project, but Becky had a visual model of all the interactions in which she had participated. What a feeling of accomplishment and what a boost to the development of her daily social skills.

Let's Play Dolls

Dolls, or in the case of a boy, cowboys or aliens, present an ideal way for us to teach our children about good friend-making behavior without having to lecture them. When we lecture, we give our child the message that what they are doing is not okay. Play acting is a very effective way to get a message across without the feel of being instructed.

When you play dolls with your child, study the way she concentrates. After a short while, you will see that your child is no longer herself but has taken on the identity of the doll who she is controlling. As you demonstrate each social behavior, your child will be taking very involved mental notes. When I played dolls with Becky, I not only spoke the appropriate words, but I discussed posture and approach. My dialogue would sound something like this. "I sit up straight and look right into your eyes so that you know I'm listening. I like your shoes," I say. "They are really pretty. I say that because I know that people like to be told what you like about them. I am being a good friend." Don't be surprised if you hear your daughter repeat, verbatim, the very words that you utter. The lesson is learned, all in the fun of play.

Let's See How Many Times I Can Succeed

We can encourage desired behavior when we keep track of the number of times the behavior occurs. Studies carried out by L. W. Frederiksen demonstrated that individuals who were prone to worry decreased the amount of their worrying when they kept track of the times they remained calm. Researchers Komaki and Dore-Boyce demonstrated that students who were known to be quiet began to speak more in class when they recorded the occurrence of their more outgoing behavior.

Taken from successes such as these, we kept track of Becky's positive social behavior in a chart. Every day, Becky placed stickers corresponding to the box that listed her good friend-making goals.

Categories included:

> Speaking to another child
> Speaking to an adult
> Smiling at another person
> Looking into a person's eyes while speaking
> Being a good listener by nodding
> Offering a snack or a toy to share

At the end of the day, Becky took pride in recording her accomplishments. The emphasis was on how Becky succeeded, and she looked forward to what she could accomplish the next day.

Give your child tangible credit for the way in which she succeeds. Be sure to list a few items that you know your child is presently capable of so that she will experience immediate success. Always remember that success breeds future success. You want your child to succeed, even if initially the accomplishments are small.

Make sure that all recording is done in a positive manner. Recording undesirable behavior will only serve to discourage and frustrate your child. Keep the thrust on the positive, and you encourage your child to increase her desirable social behaviors.

Talking on the Phone

One of my favorite techniques for enhancing my daughter's social skills came by accident. One day Becky came home from preschool determined to call another little girl in her class for a play date. Some of the children were talking about using the telephone, and Becky wanted to try, too. I asked Becky if she wanted any help, but she said that she wanted to do it herself. In a very grown-up manner, my four year old looked up the other child's name on a class list and very slowly dialed the number. The determination that was on her face faded as an adult voice answered the phone. A look of panic took over, and Becky slammed down the phone. Tears streamed down Becky's face.

When Becky calmed down enough to talk, she told me that she had planned on her little friend answering the phone. When the mother answered, Becky didn't know what to say.

As Becky spoke, I began to recall a similar situation from my childhood. I explained to Becky how, when I was about five, I called my best friend's house only to have her father answer. I also had not known what to say, and I, too, had abruptly hung up the phone. Becky and I shared feelings of disappointment, and then I told her what I had done. To assure that I would be prepared if the same situation should recur, I had written down what I wanted to say if her father answered again. Then I called back, and when he answered I was fine. Becky's face lit up. "The same thing happened to you!" she exclaimed. "I want to write down my words just like you did." Becky diligently used the same technique, and set herself up a play date for the very next day.

Aside from the success that Becky experienced that day, I learned a valuable lesson about relating to children. Following my personal rendition of a childhood event, Becky asked me day and night to tell her the same story over and over again. Becky seemed never to tire of my shared experience. It was at that moment that I realized that I had come upon an extremely useful parenting tool. We parents have a great opportunity to educate our children when we share our own life experiences with them. Children adore hearing about our childhood. Any story that I shared was accepted with delight.

If you want to make an impact upon your child, tell her about a similar incident that happened to you. She will concentrate on every word.

When I Was Your Age

Few things will capture your child's interest as much as stories from your own childhood. She will be attentive as you describe situations that you experienced as a child.

Knowledge of this response allows you to bond with your child while delivering important information without causing her to feel badly about herself. Nothing turns a child off faster than when she feels she is being told what to do.

When I had some important advice to share with Becky, I explained my suggestion by citing examples of how I faced a similar event in my own childhood.

"Oh," I might say, "I remember when I was about your age. I was at a birthday party. I didn't feel ready to sit at the party table, so I sat with my mom for a while. When a clown came out to do the show, I felt ready. I sat on the floor with the other kids. I felt so proud of myself. At the next birthday party I was ready to sit at the table."

When you share your story with your child, it is particularly helpful if you describe the situation in great detail. Children love embellished stories, and they tend to remember your message if your story includes interesting details. Whenever I used this approach, Becky would hang on my every word and, because the information was presented in story format, Becky was much more likely to remember the information that I had given her. Sharing my personal experiences with my daughter allowed us to bond in a loving way. It was not unusual for Becky to request "the story about the time you went to a birthday party," right before she was going to attend a similar event. It was as though the information I shared and the fact that I had done it, too, made it easier for Becky to do the same. My words acted as reassurance that she would also be able to handle the challenge. When you indirectly guide your child using this technique, she will come to the encouraging conclusion that "if mommy did it so can I." And, indeed, she will.

Let's Talk about Life

In order for anyone to be able to speak comfortably to others, there must be knowledge about what they are talking. This is particularly important as we attempt to increase the social successes that our child experiences. If we expose our child to a good number of activities, then it follows that she will have a wide variety of topics to talk about. Exposure to a variety of movies, music, and books will allow your child to feel comfortable speaking about these topics.

It is not unusual for the potentially social child who is making initial attempts at socialization to actually forget what it was she wanted to say. Rather than flounder for the appropriate words, Becky and I designed a notebook to assist her. Becky found it helpful to create a book where she cut out pictures of certain characters from movies or stories that she liked. She was able to refer back to this notebook whenever she wanted to refresh her memory as to what she might wish to speak about. This technique came in handy when Becky had a friend visiting, and she ran out of things to say. "Want to see my special notebook?" she would ask, and from then on the conversation would flow more easily. My inventive Becky was known to use her special book when she was talking on the phone, and she took it with her when she went visiting.

Take a Break and Ask a Question

When your child is making her initial attempts at conversation, she may find that from time to time she is at a loss for words. Becky and I discovered a wonderful technique that really helped ease the tension on occasions that this would occur. It is a known fact that most people just love to talk about themselves. Folks will tend to go on and on, often with little or no prompting. This fact comes in handy when your child needs a bit of breathing room.

When Becky felt herself running out of things to say, she would ask a question – why, how, what, or where – related to what was being discussed. This shift removed the pressure from Becky. It allowed her to concentrate and get involved in what the other person had to say. By doing so, and becoming more relaxed, Becky found that new ideas for conversation came to her. Becky learned that by shifting gears in this way she relaxed and came to enjoy the feedback the other person was giving her. She also came across as being interested in what the other person was saying—an important good friend-making behavior.

Teach your child the four question words, and she will have a tool when the need arises. As time went on and Becky became more socially comfortable, she required this technique less and less. When needed, it presented a surefire way for Becky to help herself through a potentially uncomfortable situation. Introduce your child to this easy-to-use tool, which creates a comfort zone for social success.

Making Mistakes

As a parent, we often feel that we must set a perfect example for our child. The truth is that nobody is perfect, and it is very important that your child realize this important fact.

This may be the first time you have been given this piece of advice, but I want you to let your child see you making mistakes. If this type of behavior does not naturally apply to you, then fake it. Play act if you have to. Not only do I want you to make mistakes in front of your child, but I encourage you to discuss them with her. For example: "Oh, I forgot to buy bread at the store" or "I really wanted to say hello to that lady but I didn't know what to say so I kept quiet. I'm going to say hello tomorrow."

As your child studies your reaction to your oversights and mistakes, she comes to a conclusion about her own ability to make mistakes and what exactly that means for her. If you call yourself stupid or put yourself down in any way, your child will conclude that making mistakes is not okay. If mommy does not allow herself the leeway to goof, certainly your child can't risk it either.

If you discuss that you feel annoyed at yourself and silly for not remembering something, but after all you are only human, your child will see that making mistakes is a natural way of life. When you accept yourself for not being perfect, your child will be willing to do the same for herself. The idea of "tomorrow is another day" with brand new opportunities for success is a wonderful concept for you to demonstrate to your child. She may see that you may fail today, but that just means you will try again tomorrow.

A particularly wise kindergarten teacher made mistakes on purpose so the entire class could see. She made a point of doing this so that her students would not be afraid of making mistakes themselves. If the teacher could make a mistake right in front of the class and explain it away as being an expected part of life, then it would be acceptable for children to make mistakes as well.

I urge you all to make mistakes and let your child know that it happened. Explain that you learned from your mistake, and that life goes on.

Praise to Encourage

Before we delve into a wonderful technique that will assist you in deciding upon an approach of praise for your unique child, let me share a situation where I totally blew it with Becky. On this particular day, I was given a valuable lesson I did not soon forget. I urge you to remain open minded about what your child can contribute. You may be surprised at what she has to say.

We were at my cousin's house. Becky was behaving in a particularly friendly and outgoing manner. She appeared to be having a wonderful time playing with her cousins, and I was proud of my six year old who was emerging in such a positive social way. I can't tell you why I did what I did next. Maybe my own enthusiasm got the best of me because I found myself clapping (yes, literally clapping) each time Becky entered the room. After a while, my loving and patient daughter put into words what she was feeling. "Mom, stop clapping and telling me that I am doing well. I feel embarrassed!"

Her words were uttered with the patience of a saint. I had made a mistake. Here I was, the mother who thought that she understood her child, totally forgetting what she needed, and getting carried away with my own emotions. I needed my six year old to set me straight, and she did just that. Quiet praise. I vowed that I would never again forget.

As discussed, potentially social children tend to respond best to quiet praise. That is, praise delivered to the child privately and in a way that is sincere, but not with a great deal of hoopla. Even though this is generally the case, it is important that you come to an understanding with your child regarding what, specifically, makes your child feel good. How does your child enjoy being recognized? I have compiled a list of ways that a child might feel encouraged. Add any items to this list that may come to mind. No two children are the same, and no two would respond positively to identical means of reinforcement.

I wanted Becky to let me know how she would appreciate being praised. From the items below, I asked Becky to circle the ways I could help her feel proud of her accomplishments. Becky circled the following items:

KISS ME

SMILE AT ME

WRITE A NOTE

WHISPER THAT I DID GREAT

The other items that she could have chosen
but were left uncircled:

CLAP

YELL HOORAY

GIVE A HIGH FIVE

GIVE A THUMBS UP

So often, in the case of a potentially social child, we reinforce her for desirable behavior, but, in fact, we are causing more distress than joy. Parents and teachers of such children must become aware of the ways in which a particular child likes to be praised. Praise must be tailor-made for each child so that we are sure we are delivering positive and not negative reinforcement in response to their desirable actions.

The knowledge that you gain from this exercise should be discussed with your child's teachers as well so that they know how best to comfortably praise your child.

How to Write a Love Letter

Kind words are invaluable and reinforce behavior we wish to encourage. Words of praise can be the very tool that energizes our child and gives her the confidence to go on to develop good friend-making behavior. Written form is a wonderful way to reinforce your child. From the time Becky was three, to this day, I write letters when I want to let her know she is doing a really good job.

Make a notation on your calendar every month and keep an ongoing mental note of the worthwhile behaviors that have occurred during that time. Even if your child is experimenting with some new behavior she has yet to perfect, this is a superb way to let your child know you recognize her efforts. The goal here is to write, specifically, the behavior you wish to encourage. Rather than merely writing "good job," make a point to define in very definite terms the behavior that you want to encourage.

By acknowledging your child's initial social attempts, you help her become aware of how she has progressed. Your child may not realize that the last time she was in a similar situation she did not do as well as she did today. When you point out brand new successes in written form, you help her focus on the fact that what she could not do yesterday, or last month, she can do today. What a powerful revelation for your child, and what a strong message you are sending to her about the potential for future possibilities.

So get out your pens and write your child a love letter. Be silly, loving, and fun. But most of all, let your wonderful child know just how fantastic you think she is. Through well thought out words, you give your child the impetus and courage to continue to grow!

Before you put your pen to the paper, I share one of the letters I wrote to Becky. Let my words inspire you to create a motivational letter for your child.

Dear Becky,
    I am writing to you today because I want you to know how proud I am of you.
    Last week at Aunt Paula's house, who you really don't see very much and you don't know so well, I noticed that you offered to help her set the table. That was very helpful and she told me how much she appreciated your help. I also heard you answer in a very brave, clear tone of voice when she asked you how you like school. Aunt Paula took me aside and told me how grown up she thought you were getting. You can be very proud of yourself because the last time that you visited her you did not feel ready to speak at all.

You are doing really well at using good friend-making behaviors, and I am so proud that you are my daughter. I love you very, very, very much.
Love and tons of kisses,
Mommy

It Is Not Always My Fault

It is so very important that your potentially social child realize she is not always responsible for the outcome of every social encounter. For example, let us say that your four year old gets enough courage to ask another child to play. The other child rejects her without explanation and walks away. It is not unusual for the potentially social child, who has not yet experienced much success in the social arena, to come to the swift conclusion that it was entirely her fault that the encounter ended the way that it did. This frustrated child will likely conclude that the other child did not want to play with her because she does not like her. These thoughts lead to feelings of low self worth, and if the potentially social child were to continue with this line of thinking, she may arrive at the conclusion that nobody likes her. So why should she even try? When your child takes full responsibility for any interaction, she is missing the point. We must demonstrate for our child that some things are just out of her hands.

I designed a game that illustrates this point. I use two dolls who I have converse in the following manner. One asks the other one to play. The second doll storms away without so much as a word, leaving the first doll to ponder her thoughts. I speak as though the doll is thinking. "I feel sad and left out, but it is not my fault. I was kind to her, and it is her problem, not mine, that she doesn't want to play. Maybe she didn't feel well or maybe she isn't very good at good friend-making behavior. Maybe she really doesn't like me, but that's okay, too, because not everyone can like everyone else. I know I don't like everybody. It may be that she feels unsure of herself and doesn't know what to say. I'll ask her to play once more. If she says no, I'll just forget it. There are other nice kids to play with."

Observe with delight when you see your child "get it." There will be a moment when you realize that your child understands this very important concept, and from that moment on your child will never look at a social encounter with the same amount of pressure as she had previously.

I recall an incident that occurred when I was ten that demonstrates this point. One day at school I passed another classmate in the hall. I said good morning to her, but she did not answer, and we continued past each other. I tortured myself for the rest of the morning. "She must not like me. She must think that I'm too quiet. She thinks I'm boring." My mind was filled with negative thoughts.

At lunch this same classmate approached me to apologize. "Was that you this morning who said hello," she asked. "I wasn't sure I knew you because I couldn't see too well. I forgot my glasses today and can't see more than shadows without them." I had tortured myself because I had taken full responsibility for the outcome of the encounter. It is important that we teach our child that if she has acted in a kind fashion and another individual rejects her, then it is definitely not her fault.

You Bring Something Special to Our Family

Here is a wonderful activity that involves the entire family. Instead of the traditional family tree where the names of family members are suspended from a branch of a tree, this activity stresses what it is that makes each family member special and what, particularly, that person brings to the family. A tree is drawn on a large piece of poster board. Each person is given a separate branch, and the name of that person is written on the branch itself. Along the branch various leaves are pasted below which contain the characteristics of the individual. Encourage the entire family to get involved when thinking of important ways in which each person is special. Remember to use only complimentary terms and descriptions that are accurate.

When I Help Others, I Help Myself

I have found this technique extremely successful in helping potentially social children relax. We forget our own troubles when we are concentrating on someone else. Nowhere is there a clearer demonstration of this phenomenon than with our shy child. When you find yourself and your child at a social gathering, make an attempt to notice if any other child appears to feel unsure or left out. Encourage your child to reach out.

On many occasions, I encouraged Becky to help another child feel more comfortable by sitting next to or smiling at the other child. As Becky began to concentrate on others, she focused less on her own discomfort. This activity became a game for Becky, and she was constantly on the lookout for someone else to help. She had so much fun trying to spot a child who needed kindness that she became at ease herself.

Becky became more self assured and was well liked by other children. She became known for her kindness, not her shyness.

Introduce this technique, and your child will see that other children feel unsure of themselves, too. When she focuses on others, her own anxiety will decrease. The most heartwarming side effect of this activity is that your child will be seen by herself and others as kind and friendly, and as a child who reaches out to those in need.

Try and Try Again

Success comes to those who have made numerous mistakes and, despite those setbacks, continued toward a goal. It is very important that we introduce this goal-producing concept to our potentially social child early in her life so that she may take this belief with her wherever she goes.

When your child is first introduced to the READY, SET, GO Social Readiness Program, it is likely that initially she will make little or no progress at all. Make it your business not to despair. Let your child know that instant success is not probable. Teach your child to value large and small successes, and praise your child for even minor attempts. Statements such as the following remove the pressure and go a long way to show your child that she is recognized for making any attempt at all.

"I can see that you are trying."
"I am so proud of you because you are trying."
"You must be proud of yourself
for making an attempt."

When Becky first began to attend birthday parties, she did not even want to walk through the door. This presented me with a challenging situation. How was I going to help Becky begin to feel comfortable at parties if she were unwilling to enter the room?

Upon arrival at our first few parties, Becky and I remained outside the party room for the entire time. It would have been easy for me to become totally exasperated, but I was determined to have Becky attach no negative feelings to the social event. I made conversation with Becky, discussing everything from the curtains on the windows to the songs we heard everyone else singing. When the party was over, I praised Becky for her ability to say good-bye or the way that she mouthed the words to the songs. One day when not too much behavior worthy of praise had occurred, I told Becky how well she had carried the heavy present from the car.

The point is to find something positive to comment on during the initial days of program implementation. Always begin at a point that assures your child of success, however small it may be. I counted a success with Becky to be any effort on her part that took place within the social arena. Taking a sip of soda, clapping after the birthday song, or smiling when someone looked in her direction were all opportunities for me to reinforce Becky's positive social efforts. Upon being successful in small endeavors, Becky moved on to take on more and more challenges. By showing your child that her efforts are worthwhile, however small, paves the way for future success. Be sure to let your child know it is always better to try and fail than to do nothing at all.

Not Yet

There is a three letter word that has the ability to transform your child's life. It is the word "yet." The very idea of the word yet implies possibilities. The implication is that the desired goal will eventually be reached. When we replace the self-defeating word "can't" with the inspiring term "yet," remarkable things occur for your child.

It is as though we have introduced a whole new set of opportunities, which had not existed previously. We hand our child a new set of rules where they are in charge of the timing. Consider the differences between the declarations:

"I CAN'T feel comfortable sitting at the table at the party because I am shy."
"I don't feel comfortable sitting at the table yet."

"I CAN'T call my friend on the phone."
"I haven't called my friend on the phone yet."

When we make an effort to do away with the concept of "can't" and replace this negative term with the more encouraging term "yet," possibilities for our child expand. The idea that the word "yet" conveys is that, although a particular behavior is not occurring right now, it does not mean it will not happen tomorrow.

I Am Much More Than Shy

Here is a remarkable exercise that allows your child to see her true self. Have your child lie down on a large poster board and trace the outline of her body. List as many characteristics that you can that apply to your child. Portion off various sections of the inside of your child's form, and write each of these descriptive terms within each section. Here are some ideas to get you started:

Love to draw

Funny

Loves animals

Rides bicycle well

Runs fast

Inevitably, your child will come upon a number of terms she is not particularly proud of, or that represent ways in which she has been labeled shy. When I was working on this project with Becky, she came up with these:

Don't talk in class

Play alone

Can't jump rope

Teach your child an important lesson by addressing each issue separately and discuss how else these thoughts can be expressed. This takes the idea of "yet" one step further. Work with your child to demonstrate that these thoughts can change. Here is how you can help your child rewrite these items:

Haven't talked in class yet but I will.

Still play alone but I won't always.

Haven't learned to jump rope yet but I will.

When you carry out this exercise with your child, you are teaching her many important lessons. You are helping your child get a glimpse of her future potential. You are teaching her that just because a particular skill is not yet developed does not mean that she will not be able to eventually accomplish such a goal. By helping your child look at herself in this manner, you are encouraging her to believe in the future and are letting her know you believe she can attain such goals.

This exercise gives your child a strong I CAN DO mentality. You are letting your child see for herself how much more she is than just shy. The behaviors that indicate she has challenges in the social area only comprise a very small portion of who she truly is. Potentially social children, who have been labeled as shy, very often see themselves as only shy. This exercise allows them to see themselves as much more, maybe for the very first time.

I vividly recall what Becky said as we completed this project. "Mommy, look at how much there is to me. I can do so many things!" Help your child visualize just how much good there is inside of her. Discover all that makes her unique and special. Encourage your child to see for herself all that she is capable of achieving.

Take a Vacation in Your Mind

Here is a technique that Becky invented. When working on the development of her good friend-making behaviors, there were times when she felt anxious and uncomfortable. On these occasions Becky pictured herself with her stuffed animals snuggled together in bed. After a few seconds of these thoughts, Becky felt energized to return to the task at hand. Taking a vacation in her mind by picturing herself with her favorite toys or in a favorite place helped Becky remain on course when in a challenging social situation. Help your child find something that is meaningful to her, and figure out how it can best serve her.

We all take little vacations in our mind. The ability to daydream has left many teachers wondering just how many hours their students are really in class. Our minds appear to require a bit of rest and relaxation in the midst of deep concentration.

Psychologists call these thoughts covert reinforcers. Covert reinforcers refer to private personal thoughts that bring pleasure to an individual. From ages three to six, my daughter loved to think of her Big Bird doll. She would imagine where she would go with him and what they could do. In her mind, Becky would take her stuffed animal to the beach, and they would dig at the water's edge and hold hands while running through the waves.

This imagined scene brought so much pleasure that Becky learned to reward herself for performing GFM behaviors with thoughts of her stuffed bird. As she grew older, Becky substituted thoughts of her pets or taking an imaginary trip to Grandma's.

Personal thoughts, which are enjoyable, can become a private gift to oneself as a reward for carrying out a particular behavior. This method, although only known to the individual who is using it, can be utilized from early childhood throughout old age. I still reward myself with an imaginative private vacation after I clean a closet. It encourages me to complete my goal.

Encourage your child to use this tool when she is overwhelmed by any situation. If you can teach your potentially social child to take an emotional break, she will be much more able to accomplish a challenging task. This technique allows your child to take care of herself for the rest of her life.

EPILOGUE

I began this book with the story of a shy little girl who believed that she COULD NOT behave in a social manner. Fortunately for me, I was able to find my way, but it was not easy.

Throughout the book, I shared with you techniques that foster social success. When we create an environment in which our child comes to believe in her social self, then social comfort becomes a reality.

Now that my words are coming to an end, I extend an invitation to each of you. Please write and let me know what you have found to be beneficial in support of your potentially social child. I look forward to hearing from you.

Every day, let your child know that you believe she CAN!

Share your thoughts and feelings with other parents, teachers, and shy adults.
Visit the website at www.dontcallmeshy.com
or
contact Laurie Adelman personally at
Laurie@dontcallmeshy.com

APPENDIX

To Teachers of Shy Children

Teachers are in a unique position to have a major impact upon shy children. These children spend much of their day with you, and it is you who, firsthand, witness the social difficulties these children have. Teachers, never underestimate your ability to help bring out the social best in your students who are shy!

Shy children pose a challenge to teachers in the classroom. In many cases, you are aware that a shy student knows the answer but appears to be unwilling to express herself. In fact, the child is not unwilling—she is unable.

The goal you have for many of your shy students is to speak in class and reach out to fellow students and make friends. This goal is not attainable until a shy child is helped to believe she has this ability in the first place. Here's where an insightful teacher can make a real difference in how far a shy student progresses. The story of Eleanor Roosevelt (chapter 4) is likely to touch your heart as you read about the immense influence a caring, knowledgeable teacher had upon the social development of this strong political leader who was once extremely shy. This story highlights the fact that teachers have a lot to do with how much a shy child's social potential is realized.

If you are in search of an approach to help shy children successfully function in school you will find the methods discussed throughout the book easily applicable to the classroom. Read each chapter carefully and familiarize yourself with the factors that help determine how and why a shy child behaves the way she does. Focus on the Skill Builders, and you will find that most are conducive to classroom use. These techniques will not only help the shy children in your class—they will be beneficial to all of your students, no matter what their level of social ability.

On the following pages is a **Lesson Plan for Teachers: to bring out the social best in shy students.**

Lesson Plan for Teachers
To bring out the social best in shy students

Subject:

The participation and comfort level of shy children at school.

Grades:

Preschool-Grade12

Brief Description:

Shy children have a difficult time participating in class and initiating interaction with the teacher and other students. The words and actions of the teacher can encourage participatory behavior and build social skills.

Objective:

To increase the confidence and visibility of shy children at school. Shy students will increase the number of times that they volunteer to contribute in class, and will become active members of their class and school. These children will feel more comfortable in the classroom and will reach out to others and make friends, in class and during recess.

Thought Process:

A shy child's beliefs about herself keep her shy. When a shy child is given the opportunity to participate and succeed in a social situation, even minimally, she begins to believe that she has the ability to achieve social success - and she is more likely to make further social attempts.

The Lesson:

The lesson is on-going. Every day teacher will institute one or more of the following:

- Avoid using the word "shy" when referring to child or behavior
- Use puppets/and or role play to demonstrate good friend-making behavior
- Student will hand out items in class (papers, crayons, snacks)
- Student will be given leadership positions that are non-threatening(dismissing the class, instructing classmates to line up for lunch)
- During class time: Student will be quietly recognized for any social gesture or voluntary participation
- After class: Student will be given positive feedback in notes and private discussions to recognize social and participatory behavior
- Teacher will make mistakes in class on purpose to create relaxed environment and to demonstrate that everyone makes mistakes and nobody can expect to be perfect

Assessment:

Did shy students increase their contribution in class?
Did students make friends?
Was there an increase in comfort level of child in school?

Rationale:

These techniques will increase the participation and comfort level of all children, regardless of their social ability. Giving a child a job in class puts the child in control and increases their status in the classroom, in their own eyes and in the eyes of others. When a shy child is put in charge of a situation, she gains recognition and importance in a non-threatening way.

Biblical Meditation

Meditation is the process of deep thinking on the truths and spiritual realities revealed in Scripture for the purposes of understanding, application, and prayer.

- Choose the verse(s), phrase, or word that impresses you most during your encounter with Scripture
  - Find a verse that relates to your personal need or concern
  - Discern the main message of the section of your reading and meditate on its meaning
- Repeat the text in different ways
  - Examine the verse from every facet, repeating the verse to emphasize each word & consider its meaning
- Rewrite it in your own words
- Look for applications for the text
  - "How am I to respond to this text?"
- Pray through the text
  - This is an invitation for the Holy Spirit to hold His divine light over the words of Scripture to show you what you can't see without Him
- Consider cross references that relate to your chosen text

Teacher recognition and positive feedback will increase the occurrence of the behavior that is being recognized. Be careful to offer quiet praise to shy children. Loud praise tends to embarrass these children.

Follow-up:

Incorporate lesson plan into class routine on a continuous basis, fine-tuning methods as needed. Refer to Skill Builders (*Don't Call Me Shy*, chapter 14) to create additional lesson plans. Discuss child's progress with parents and encourage family to use the same techniques at home.

© Laurie Adelman. *Don't Call Me Shy*, 2007

Words of Encouragement for Shy Adults

Although this book is geared to parenting and teaching shy children, all of the information and techniques pertain to shy adults as well. During your own childhood you formed a social belief system with the message that you were shy. As a result, you have come to the conclusion that you are unable to behave any other way. The exercises in this book will help you realize how the way you define yourself directly translates into the expectations that you have of yourself. We are going to change those expectations and, as a result, change the way that you behave.

Read each chapter carefully and take your time to absorb the information. You will need to parent yourself. It is not easy, but it can be done. That is how I transformed myself from a shy child and adolescent into a socially comfortable adult.

If possible, reach out to a family member or a friend and ask them to help you. Allow this person to take on the role of your parent and assist you in carrying out the exercises and giving you the feedback that you need.

Take one day at a time and give yourself credit for making an effort. Be proud of every step you take, even if it seems you are making minimal progress at first. You need to experience small social successes before you will feel confident to move on to bigger challenges. And with each passing day you will prove to yourself and others that you CAN behave in a socially comfortable manner.

SUPPLEMENTAL READING

CHAPTER 4

Gilbert, M., *Shy Girl*, New York: Doubleday & Company, Inc., 1965. (Roosevelt)

Kagan, Jerome, et al., "Childhood derivatives of inhibition and lack of inhibition to the unfamiliar." *Child Development;* v59, n6, 1580-1589, Dec. 1988.

Kagan, Jerome, Snidman, N., "Tempermental factors in human development." *American Psychologist.* V46, n8, 856-862, Aug. 1991.

CHAPTER 6

Jahoda, Gustav, "A note on Ashanti names and relation to personality." *British Journal of Psychology,* 45:192-195, 1054.

Jemmott, J.B. and Gonzalez, E., "Social status and the status distribution and performance in small groups." *Journal of Applied Social Psychology.* 19, 584-596, 1989.

Luria, A., *The Role of Speech in the Regulaton of Normal and Abnormal Bdehaviors.* New York: Liveright, 1961. (Sagan, Rogers, Adler)

Vygotsky, L.S., *Thought and Language* (E. Hantmann and G. Vokar Eds and Trans.) Cambridge, Mass M.1.1 Press, 1965. (Sagan, Rogers, Adler)

Vygotsky, L.S., *Mind in Society: the development of higher psychological processes* (M. Cole et al, Eds) Cambridge Mass: Howard University Press, 1978.

CHAPER 7

Hymal, S, Rubin, K.H., Rowden, L., "Children's peer relationships." *Child Development.* 61, 2004-2021, 1990.

Richmond, V.P., Beatty, M.J., Dyba, P., "Shyness and Popularity: Children's views." *Western Journal of Speech Communication,* 49, 116-125, 1985.

Rubin, K.H., Hymal, S., Mills, R., "Sociability and social withdrawal in childhood stability and outcomes." *Journal of Personality,* 57, 237-255, 1989.

Rubin, K.H., Mills, R.S.L., "The many faces of social isolation in childhood." *Journal of Consulting and Clinical Psychology.* 56, 916-924, 1988.

Turner, S.M., Beidel, D.C., Jacob, R.G., "Social Phobia." *Journal of Counseling and Clinical Psychology,* 62, 350-358, 1994.

Younger, A.J., Schwartzman, A.E., Ledingham, J.E., "Age related changes in children's perceptions of aggression and withdrawal in their peers," *Developmental Psychology*, 21, 70-75, 1985.

CHAPTER 9

Gunnar, M., "Psychoendocrine studies of temperament and stress in early childhood," *Temperment: Individual Differences at the Interface of Biology and Behavior*, (J. Bates and T. Wachs, ed), Washington, D.C., American Psychological Press, 1994.

Gunnar, M., et al, "The Stressfulness of Separation Among Nine-Month-Old Infants." *Child Development*, 1992.

Hilgard, E., Atkinson, R., *Introduction to Psychology*, 6th ed. New York: Harcourt Brace Jovanovitch, 1975.

Jones, M.C, "Elimination of children's fears," *Journal of Experimental Psychology*, 1924, 381-390.

Mineka, S, Zinbarg, R., Animal modes of pathopathology, In C.E Walker (ED) *Clinical Psychology-Historical and Research Foundations*, Plenum Press, 1991, 51-86.

Mineka s, Zinbarg R., Conditioning and ethological models of social phobia. In R.G. Heimberg, M.R. Liebowitz, D.A. Hope, and F.R. Schneier (EDS), *Social Phobia – Diagnosis, assessment, and treatment*, N.Y Guilford Press, 1995, 134-162.

Ost, L.G., "Ways of acquiring phobias and outcome of behavioral treatments," *Behavior Research and Therapy*, 1985, 23, 683-9.

Watson, J.B., "Conditional emotional reactions," *Journal of Experimental Psychology*, 1920, 3, 1-14.

CHAPTER 10

Alexander, P.A., "Coming to terms," *Review of Educational Research*, 61, 315-43, 1991.

Barrett, P.M., "Family intervention for childhood anxiety," *Journal of Consulting and Clinical Psychology*, 1996, 64, 333-42

Burke, L.W., "Effects of Communal Rearing in Synanon," DHEW grant proposal 1975.

Caudill, W.A., "General Culture," *The Journal of Nervous and Mental Disease*, 1973, 157, 240-57.

Caudill, W.A., Schooler, C., "Child Behavior and Child Rearing in Japan and the U.S." *Journal of Nervous and Mental Disease*, 1973, 157, 240-257.

Dworetzky, J.P., *Introduction To Child Development*, New York: McMillian, 1996. (Bijou)

Gredler, M.E., *Learning and Instruction Theory into Practice*, New York: McMillian, 1980. (Bijou)

Jarus, A., Marcus J., Oren J., *Children and Families in Israel: Some Mental Health Perspectives*, New York: Gordon and Breach, 1970.

Kirby, F.D., Toler H.C., "Modification of preschool isolate behavior-case study," *Journal of Applied Behavior Analysis*, 1970, 3, 309-14.

Missakian, E.A., "Social Behavior of Communally-Reared Children," Department of Health, Education and Welfare grant proposal, 1976.

Simon, S.I., "The Synanon Game," *Dissertation Abstracts International*, 36, 1975.

Watson, J.B., "Conditional emotional reactions," *Journal of Experimental Psychology*, 1920, 3, 1-14.

Watson, John B., *Psychological Care of Infant and Child*, New York, W.W. Norton, 1928.

Chapter 13

Goldfried, M.R., Anxiety Reduction, in P.C. Kendall and S.D. Hollen, *Cognitive-Behavioral Interventions: Theory, Research, and Procedures*, Academic Press: New York, 1979.

Perri, M.G, Richards, C.S., "An investigation of naturally occurring episodes." *Journal of Counseling Psychology*, 1977, 24, 178-83.

Rubin, L., Social withdrawal in childhood, in S.R. Asher and J.D. Coie (eds.) *Peer Rejection in Childhood*, Cambridge England: Cambridge University Press, 1990.

Vernberg, E.M., Abwender, D.A., Ewell K.K., Beery S.H., "Social Anxiety and Peer Relationships in Early Adolescents," *Journal of Clinical Child Psychology*, 1992, 21, 189-96.

Watson, D.L. and Tharp, R.G., *Self-Directed Behavior*, Brooks/Cole Publishing Company: Monterey, California, 1981.

Chapter 14

Cavatela, J.R., "Covert Processes," *Journal of Nervous and Mental Diseases*, 1973, 157, 27-36. (Covert reinforcers)

Frederiksen, L.W., "Treatment of ruminative thinking by self monitoring." *Journal of Behavior Therapy and Experimental Psychiatry*, 1975, 6, 258-9.

Komaki, J, Dore-Boyce K., "Self recording – its effect on individual's high and low in motivation," *Behavior Therapy*, 1978, 9, 65-72.

Kirby, F.D., Toler H.C., "Modification of preschool isolate behavior-case study," *Journal of Applied Behavior Analysis*, 1970, 3, 309-14.

About the Author

Laurie Adelman is a nurse and health educator, a shyness life coach, and a child advocate who is passionately devoted to teaching parents and teachers how to interact with shy children in a way that brings out a child's social best.

Ms. Adelman earned a B.S.N. in Community Health and a M.S. in Family Health and Health Education. She was recognized with honors for writing a thesis on learning theory in which she described a method enabling individuals to retain information and incorporate new skills into everyday life.

Laurie Adelman has written numerous educational and inspirational articles, newsletters, brochures, and medical abstracts. She has designed and carried out many education programs for children and adults and received an award for Outstanding Contributions in Health Education.

The study of shyness has been a passion of Ms. Adelman for more than 25 years. She writes straight from the heart, sharing personal experiences from her own life while enriching her descriptions with the stories of others.

Ms. Adelman is on a mission to help each and every shy child shine in their own special way, given the opportunity to achieve a level of social comfort of which that they can be proud.

— To Order —
Don't Call Me Shy
by Laurie Adelman

If this book is not available at your local bookstore,
LangMarc Publishing will fill your order
within 48 hours.

LangMarc Publishing
P.O. Box 90488 • Austin, Texas 78709
or call 1-800-864-1648
or order www.langmarc.com

or contact Laurie Adelman at
Laurie@dontcallmeshy.com

$14.95 U.S.A. or $17.95 Canada

Please send me _____ copies of
Don't Call Me Shy at $14.95 each   _____
Tax Texas residents only 8.15%   _____
Shipping 1 book $3.00; $1 each   _____
    additional book
Total cost: _____

Shipping address:
Your name   _____
Your address   _____

_____

Billing Address: (same?)   _____
Credit card (or check)   _____
_____ Expiration: _____